T0322917

TOO EASY
Copyright © Donna Hay Pty Ltd 2024
Design copyright © Donna Hay Pty Ltd 2024
Photography copyright © Con Poulos 2024
Recipes and styling: Donna Hay
Art direction and design: Genevieve McKelvey
Art director and managing editor: Hannah Schubert
Copy editor: Pru Engel
Senior recipe tester: Jacinta Cannataci
Recipe kitchen assistant: Olivia Pollock
Studio assistant: William Davidson

The rights of Donna Hay to be identified as the author and Con Poulos as the photographer of
this work have been asserted by them under the *Copyright Amendment (Moral Rights) Act 2000*.
This work is copyright. Apart from any use as permitted under the *Copyright Act 1968*, no part
may be reproduced, copied, scanned, stored in a retrieval system, recorded or transmitted,
in any form or by any means, without the prior written permission of the publisher.
Without limiting the author's and publisher's exclusive rights, any unauthorised use of this
publication to train generative artificial intelligence (AI) technologies is expressly prohibited.

Fourth Estate
An imprint of HarperCollins*Publishers*

HarperCollins*Publishers*
Australia • Brazil • Canada • France • Germany • Holland • India
Italy • Japan • Mexico • New Zealand • Poland • Spain • Sweden
Switzerland • United Kingdom • United States of America

HarperCollins acknowledges the Traditional Custodians of the lands upon
which we live and work, and pays respect to Elders past and present.

First published on Gadigal Country in Australia in 2024
by HarperCollins*Publishers* Australia Pty Limited
ABN 36 009 913 517
harpercollins.com.au

A catalogue record for this book is available from the National Library of Australia
ISBN 978 1 4607 6634 7 (paperback)
ISBN 978 1 4607 1775 2 (ebook)

Reproduction by Hannah Schubert, Genevieve McKelvey and Splitting Image
Printed and bound in China
6 5 4 3 2 1   24 25 26 27 28

too easy

**All the simple shortcuts you need,
for all the delicious food you want**

FOURTH ESTATE

contents

too easy!

All the **simple shortcuts** you need,
for all the **delicious food** you want

What's for dinner...?

Your weeknight dinner repertoire is set for a shake-up!

The recipes in this book seriously **deliver on flavour**, transforming a few pantry staples and fresh ingredients into **delicious meals within minutes**.

Here you'll find clever updates on **classics you love**, the easiest **toss-together dinners**, and my spin on recipes for your **air fryer:** they're lightning-fast, super tasty and big on crispy, golden crunch.

My go-to **one-pan wonders** and new ways with **powerhouse pantry ingredients** give you even more tasty switch-ups to put on high rotation. And whether you're cooking for family or entertaining, my genius **set-and-forget** recipes will take the pressure off while your oven does all the work.

I haven't forgotten those sweet cravings, so there are also my completely **irresistible snacks** and effortlessly **impressive desserts** that I know you'll love.

With so many inspiring, no-fuss ideas, dinner never looked so good, **or so easy**! Enjoy!

pantry *staples*

One thing I'm always asked is, what are my *favourite things* to keep in the pantry? I like to be *ready for any meal* or occasion – even if it's just a last-minute *weeknight dinner*. Here's a list of what I like to keep on hand. My advice is to always have the things that will help you create your *go-to dishes* and most-loved flavour combos.

Basics

My list of must-haves: the things that make me feel like I can always create a quick dinner solution.

pasta
Thin linguine or spaghetti, risoni and a tube-style pasta such as rigatoni or penne.

rice
I always have jasmine, basmati and brown on hand - they're versatile in a range of dishes. Carnaroli is my favourite for risotto.

grains
Quinoa, freekeh and cracked wheat for robust, nutritious salads.

canned and dried pulses
My faves are chickpeas, lentils, black beans and creamy butter beans. They're a great shortcut base for salads, soups and stews.

canned tomatoes, passata and concentrated paste
In my pantry: all of them, always! Canned whole peeled, cherry and chopped are a must, as is a passata or purée and a thick tomato paste. These are the building blocks for so many dishes.

oils and vinegars
A good-quality extra virgin olive oil; mild-flavoured for frying and baking; fruity for dressings; a vegetable or grapeseed oil for baking. Wine vinegars for dressings; rice wine vinegar for Asian; balsamic for everything.

Fridge

For me, a well-stocked fridge is the difference between a great meal and a good one.

lemons and limes
My life is not complete if I don't have at least a lemon or two in the fridge. Limes run a close second. Wash them under hot water before using.

fresh herbs
Mint and basil are my go-tos for freshening up dishes. I store them in water in the fridge, or wrapped in damp absorbent kitchen paper to help them last longer.

cheeses
You can never have too many in my opinion! I usually have parmesan, cheddar, feta, soft goat's cheese, haloumi and mascarpone.

yoghurt and cream
A great thick Greek yoghurt is useful for savoury dishes, plus it's one of my favourite baking ingredients. Cream is a great standby ingredient: splash into a pasta sauce or use as the foundation of a quick dessert.

dips
Keep a variety on standby as they are great to serve as a side or snack at a moment's notice. Hummus and tzatziki are faves.

unsalted butter for baking
It's worth spending a little extra on good-quality butter for baking, as it will give the tastiest results. Not all butters are equal!

Freezer

I think of my freezer as the greatest stand-by second pantry, only chillier.

peas, spinach and edamame beans
Three of the greats that can add that green pop of creaminess and goodness.

puff and shortcrust pastry
If you have pastry, you can make so many things, from a throw-together lunch tart to a speedy but glam cheat's dessert.

vanilla bean ice-cream
Because everything is better with ice-cream (and see my impressive dessert on p198).

raspberries, blueberries, mango
Not just for smoothies, these are great for baking, simple snacks and desserts.

fresh breadcrumbs
I blitz fresh sourdough bread to make a few batches at once, then freeze in small bags so I always have some on hand.

cooked rice
Small portions of cooked frozen rice are handy dinner starters: think fried rice or rice omelette, or simply serve as a side dish.

Thai lime leaves
These little leaves are vital when you want to add a burst of Thai flavour. I can't always get to the Asian grocer so, when I can, I buy extra and freeze them.

chips and french fries
Because sometimes you just need that crisp, salty crunch.

Baking

Using quality ingredients makes all the difference when you're baking.

nuts
Essential for flavour and crunch as well as keeping bakes moist and tender. Ground almonds (almond meal) is a must.

dried fruits
These can add a pop of sweetness to salads, muffins and bakes.

flours
My essentials include plain, rice, cornflour and buckwheat.

sugars
Different sugars give different flavours and outcomes in baking. I have caster, icing, brown and coconut sugar as my staples.

vanilla
A good-quality extract and beans are a must for me. I can't bake without them.

cocoa powder
As a guide, the higher percentage of fat in the cocoa, the richer and better-quality the flavour will be.

good-quality baking chocolate
If you want great-tasting chocolate desserts and cake, you need to start with a great chocolate. Dark should be 70% cocoa solids.

honey and maple syrup
These two are my favourite sweeteners. Use pure maple syrup and a pure honey for the best flavour.

Sauces

A drizzle of a flavourful sauce or syrup can uplift a huge variety of dishes from various cuisines.

hoisin
This rich, sweet and salty sauce is a great base for many Asian-inspired dishes, from stir-fries to dumplings and meatballs.

mirin (Japanese rice wine)
A slightly sweet and tangy rice wine, great for marinades and sauces.

pomegranate molasses
This rich, thick, tart and tangy syrup is a game changer. It can lift a simple salad dressing or add depth and tangy sweetness to slow-simmered lamb. Experiment at will!

fish sauce
A versatile ingredient that adds punchy umami seasoning to a range of dishes.

chilli sauce
So many to choose from – maybe too many! It's a game of discovery and adventure, so start tasting and then return to the types that suit your taste and heat tolerance.

soy
A great soy sauce goes a long way to add rich colour and flavour. You may like to keep a couple of variations – light, dark or sweet – depending on the depth of flavour you need.

Pastes

Perfect for marinades, sauces, dressings and more.

harissa
A sweet, deeply rich and mild chilli paste with garlic and spices like cumin and coriander. Use it to add a complex, subtle heat and flavour to soups, slow cooks, dressings, marinades and more.

gochujang
This Korean staple is so much more than a chilli paste. It adds heat but it's also savoury and slightly sweet.

miso
This fermented paste can be used in lots of different ways to add serious depth of flavour. I like to use it in marinades.

wasabi
It's not just for sushi! Add this vibrant paste to dressings, mash and sauces for a zippy little zing.

chipotle in adobo
These smoke-dried jalapeño chillies are best purchased in the rich, earthy adobo sauce. I like to mash the chipotle chillies into the adobo sauce before using.

curry pastes
Curry pastes are great for so much more than use in a traditional curry. Think outside the box, as they can add a big flavour burst to dishes such as burgers, stir-fries and fish cakes.

Spices + blends

There are so many great spices and combinations to choose from, but these are my current top five.

smoked paprika

A simple way to add a sweet smokiness to so many things, including sauces, marinades, dressings and salsas.

Chinese five-spice

This spice mix is one of my secret weapons. A simple shake adds so much depth of flavour to many Asian dishes and foods such as fried chicken or simmered meats.

ras el hanout

This 'house blend' of aromatic spices includes sweet paprika, cumin, cinnamon, coriander, turmeric, pepper and more. My favourite way to use it is to sprinkle over vegetables before roasting or grilling.

shichimi togarashi

This Japanese seven-spice blend is a versatile condiment, great for sprinkling over noodle dishes, vegetables or salads for a spicy, nutty, umami-packed finishing touch.

Sichuan peppercorns

I find these piquant little peppercorns super addictive. The numbing spice and tongue-tingling zing is unique and always has you coming back for more.

Condiments

Condiments and pickles are good for so much more than serving on the side. They're superstar stand-bys that add serious punch.

mustard

Mustards can rescue anything bland and give it a new life. I use them in dressings, marinades or sauces for extra punch. I love the creamy hit of dijon mustard the most.

chutney and relish

My must-haves include caramelised onion, spicy mango and a good balsamic tomato relish. These little jars of wonder can save a bland dish with just a few spoonfuls.

crispy chilli oil

I like mine to be packed with flavour, not just heat. Add to everything and anything from scrambled eggs to chicken burgers. See my website for a great recipe.

pickled ginger

I reach for this jar so often! I like to shred the ginger and toss it through salads or rice. It also makes a great ginger mayo for sandwiches and burgers.

kimchi and sauerkraut

I group these zippy ferments together as I use them in a similar fashion. Add to wellness bowls and salads, or to a toasted cheese sandwich or burger.

capers

Hands-down my fave! They're great when fresh or fried, and for adding a crisp tang to salads and pastas.

faster than *takeaway*

If you're pushed for time and *inspiration,* ordering takeaway for dinner is a handy go-to. I promise, though, that my easy homemade versions of *takeaway favourites* will deliver on flavour, *transforming* a few pantry staples and fresh ingredients into *speedy and satisfying meals within minutes.*

These super-quick
toss-together dinners
are so simple and
delicious, they will
easily become a
new staple in your
weeknight repertoire.

in this chapter

Don't be fooled into thinking a *delicious pad thai* needs a list of ingredients as long as your arm. My version is a simple *combination of flavours* that delivers serious yum factor.

chicken pad thai

300g (10½ oz) dried rice noodles
2 tablespoons vegetable oil
1 brown onion, cut into thin wedges
3 x 180g (6½ oz) chicken breast fillets, trimmed and sliced
3 eggs, lightly whisked
2 cups (160g/5½ oz) bean sprouts
4 green onions (scallions), thinly sliced
½ cup (70g/2½ oz) chopped roasted cashews
thinly sliced long red chilli and lime wedges, to serve
pad thai sauce
⅓ cup (80g/2¾ oz) firmly packed brown sugar
⅓ cup (80ml/2½ fl oz) fish sauce
⅓ cup (80ml/2½ fl oz) white vinegar
2 tablespoons tomato paste (concentrated purée)

To make the pad thai sauce, combine the sugar, fish sauce, vinegar and tomato paste in a small saucepan over medium–high heat. Bring to a rapid simmer and cook, stirring occasionally, for 5 minutes or until the sauce has thickened slightly.

Cook the noodles according to the packet instructions. Refresh under cold water, drain and set aside.

Heat a large deep frying pan or wok over high heat.

Add the oil and onion and cook for 2–3 minutes or until the edges are charred.

Add the chicken and cook, stirring, for 3 minutes or until cooked through. Move the chicken and onion to one side of the pan.

On the other side of the pan, add the egg and, without stirring, cook for 30 seconds. Add the noodles and toss everything to combine.

Add the bean sprouts, green onion and pad thai sauce and toss to combine.

Serve with cashews, chilli and lime wedges. **SERVES 4**

Cook's note: You can switch up this recipe and swap the chicken for peeled raw prawns, chopped firm tofu or thinly sliced beef.

This super-easy *flavour-packed* dinner is ready in a flash. With just a few *simple ingredients,* it's *everything you love* about Indian-style takeaway but better (not to mention, quicker)!

butter chicken naan breads

¼ cup (70g/2½ oz) store-bought butter chicken curry paste
500g (1 lb 2 oz) chicken mince
¼ cup (70g/2½ oz) store-bought mango chutney, plus extra to serve
4 store-bought naan bread, warmed
½ cup (125g/4½ oz) plain thick Greek yoghurt
thinly sliced long green chilli and coriander (cilantro) leaves, to serve

Heat a large non-stick frying pan over medium–high heat.

Add the curry paste and cook for 30 seconds or until fragrant. Add the chicken and cook for 5 minutes, breaking up any large lumps with a wooden spoon.

Add the mango chutney and cook for 1 minute.

Spread each naan bread with yoghurt. Top with the butter chicken mince, extra mango chutney, chilli and coriander to serve. **SERVES 4**

Cook's note: Swap the chicken mince for lamb, beef or pork mince or try finely chopped firm tofu for a vegetarian option. To warm the naan breads, pop them in the microwave or warm in a dry pan over medium heat for a few seconds – too easy!

My version of this classic ticks the box for a speedy dinner because you cook it *just like a stir fry*. It's packed with all the flavour and textures you want in a green curry, only it's *ready in no time!*

quick green chicken curry

1 tablespoon vegetable oil
1 brown onion, cut into wedges
¼ cup (75g/2¾ oz) store-bought Thai green curry paste
400ml (13½ fl oz) coconut cream
4 x 180g (6½ oz) chicken breast fillets, trimmed and cut into chunks
300g (10½ oz) green beans, trimmed and chopped
225g (8 oz) can bamboo shoots, drained
⅓ cup (17g/½ oz) chopped coriander (cilantro) leaves
steamed rice, extra coriander (cilantro) sprigs and lime wedges, to serve

Heat a large deep frying pan or wok over medium–high heat.

Add the oil and onion and cook for 4 minutes. Add the curry paste and cook for 1 minute or until fragrant.

Add the coconut cream and bring to a simmer. Add the chicken and beans and cook for 4–5 minutes or until cooked. Add the bamboo shoots and coriander and stir to combine.

Serve with rice, extra coriander and lime wedges. **SERVES 4**

Cook's note: This recipe is such a favourite as it is so versatile. You can switch up the chicken for firm tofu and the beans for any veg you have in the fridge.

This is truly the most *comforting, satisfying* dinner. The trick is simmering the gnocchi in milk, which creates a *delightfully creamy* sauce for a one-pan wonder that never fails to impress.

spinach and mozzarella gnocchi

3½ cups (875ml/29½ fl oz) milk
800g (1 lb 12 oz) store-bought potato gnocchi
280g (10 oz) baby spinach leaves
1 cup (80g/2¾ oz) finely grated parmesan
2 teaspoons finely grated lemon rind
sea salt and cracked black pepper
2 x 125g (4½ oz) fresh mozzarella, drained well and torn

Place the milk in a deep ovenproof frying pan and bring to a simmer. Add the gnocchi and cook for 3 minutes or until just soft.

Preheat oven grill (broiler) to high.

Stir through the baby spinach, ¾ cup (60g/2 oz) of the parmesan, lemon rind, salt and pepper.

Top with the mozzarella and remaining parmesan.

Grill for 8–10 minutes or until golden and serve. **SERVES 4**

Cook's note: Whatever type of gnocchi you choose, cook it until it is just soft – overcooked gnocchi gets a little soggy! Any type of greens will work here, too, such as shredded kale, silverbeet or frozen peas.

Who wouldn't want *hot, crispy pizza* in 15 minutes flat? Sure, the takeaway option seems appealing, until it arrives soggy and a little cold, that is! Try my version instead – it's a cinch to prepare and *never disappoints* on molten cheesy, crunchy deliciousness.

chorizo and zucchini pizza

2 large flatbreads
½ cup (125ml/4 fl oz) tomato passata (purée)
1 zucchini (courgette), thinly sliced lengthways
2 cups (70g/2½ oz) firmly packed shredded kale leaves (about 2 stalks kale)
2 chorizo (200g/7 oz), sliced
1 tablespoon oregano leaves
2 x 125g (4½ oz) fresh mozzarella, drained well and torn
extra virgin olive oil, for drizzling
finely grated parmesan, to serve

Preheat oven to 240°C (475°F). Place two baking trays in the oven to preheat for 10 minutes.

Place each flatbread on a sheet of non-stick baking paper. Spread each flatbread with half the passata and top with the zucchini, kale, chorizo, oregano and mozzarella.

Drizzle each pizza with oil. Place on the hot preheated trays and cook for 12–15 minutes or until golden.

Sprinkle with parmesan and slice to serve. **MAKES 2 PIZZAS**

Cook's note: It's super easy to use this base pizza recipe to make a pizza with whichever toppings you love. From a classic margherita to wherever your taste buds take you – make it your own.

This pasta dish has become one of the *most-requested lunches* in the dh studio – it's now a treasured favourite! The key is the perfect balance of *fresh basil and creamy tomato* goodness.

creamy sundried tomato rigatoni

500g (1 lb 2 oz) dried rigatoni
¾ cup (180g/6½ oz) thinly sliced semi sundried tomatoes
¼ cup (65g/2 oz) tomato paste (concentrated purée)
1½ cups (375ml/12½ fl oz) pure (pouring) cream
sea salt and cracked black pepper
1 cup (20g/¾ oz) basil leaves
¾ cup (60g/2 oz) finely grated parmesan, plus extra to serve (optional)

Cook the pasta in a large saucepan of boiling salted water until al dente. Drain, reserving ½ cup (125ml/4 fl oz) of the pasta water.

While the pasta is cooking, place a large deep non-stick frying pan over medium heat. Add the sundried tomatoes and tomato paste and cook for 1 minute or until fragrant.

Add the cream, salt and pepper and bring to a simmer. Add the pasta, reserved pasta water and cook for 1 minute, stirring, or until the pasta is well coated. Remove from the heat.

Add the basil and parmesan and mix to combine.

Divide between bowls and serve with extra parmesan, if desired. **SERVES 4**

Cook's note: Swap the rigatoni for 400g penne or your favourite pasta shape. The secret to nailing this dish is to add enough pasta water to make a light, velvety cream sauce that just coats the pasta.

Move over croutons... *haloumi crisps* are the new super-easy way to add *cheesy, salty crunch.* They transform this clever salad of humble frozen peas into the most *elegantly irresistible* dish.

smashed pea and prosciutto salad with haloumi crisps

300g (10½ oz) haloumi, shaved using a vegetable peeler
60g (2 oz) unsalted butter
500g (1 lb 2 oz) frozen peas
2 teaspoons finely grated lemon rind
sea salt and cracked black pepper
1½ cups (24g/1 oz) mint leaves
150g (5½ oz) rocket (arugula) leaves
8 slices prosciutto
toasted bread slices and lemon wedges, to serve

Preheat oven to 160°C (325°F).

To make the haloumi crisps, spread the haloumi on a large tray lined with non-stick baking paper and bake for 10–12 minutes or until golden and crisp.

Heat a large frying pan over medium heat. Add the butter and cook until melted. Add the peas, lemon rind, salt and pepper and stir to combine. Cook for 2–3 minutes or until the peas are heated through.

Using a fork, roughly smash half the peas. Add the mint and rocket and toss to combine.

Divide the bread slices between serving plates. Top with the smashed peas, prosciutto, haloumi and serve with lemon wedges.
SERVES 4

Cook's note: To ensure a crispy haloumi, it needs to be sliced super thinly – a vegetable peeler does the job easily. You can change up the prosciutto for rashers of crispy bacon if you prefer.

The secret to a great poke bowl is layers of *colour, texture and crunch,* enhanced with generous splashes of a seriously good dressing. My *miso tahini dressing* meets the brief – you'll love it!

simple poke bowl with miso tahini dressing

4 cups (660g/1 lb 7 oz) cooked brown rice

2 cups (180g/6½ oz) finely shredded red cabbage

1½ cups (240g/8½ oz) frozen shelled edamame (green soy beans), blanched and cooled

3 carrots, peeled and shredded using a julienne peeler

350g (12½ oz) smoked trout fillets

⅓ cup (30g/1 oz) store-bought pickled ginger

store-bought sliced pickled red onion and furikake, to serve

miso tahini dressing

⅓ cup (80ml/2½ fl oz) rice wine vinegar

⅓ cup (80ml/2½ fl oz) sesame oil

⅓ cup (120g/4½ oz) honey

2 tablespoons white miso paste

2 tablespoons hulled tahini

To make the miso tahini dressing, whisk together the rice wine vinegar, sesame oil, honey, miso and tahini.

To assemble the poke bowl, divide the rice between bowls.

Top with cabbage, edamame, carrot, smoked trout, pickled ginger and pickled red onion. Sprinkle with furikake and serve. **SERVES 4**

Cook's note: You can switch up this recipe and use smoked salmon slices or sashimi – tuna, salmon or kingfish would all work well – or sliced cooked chicken instead of the trout. Permission to use store-bought cooked rice is granted!

This is my cheat's version of the *takeaway favourite,* gozleme.
You can throw it together in around 20 minutes and it's the perfect
combination of spice, crunch and *melty, cheesy* goodness.

harissa-spiced beef flatbreads

2 tablespoons extra virgin olive oil, plus extra for brushing
3 cloves garlic, thinly sliced
500g (1 lb 2 oz) beef mince
1 tablespoon harissa paste
1 cup (120g/4½ oz) grated carrot
2 teaspoons smoked paprika
1 tablespoon tomato paste (concentrated purée)
¼ cup (13g/½ oz) chopped flat-leaf (Italian) parsley leaves
sea salt and cracked black pepper
2 large round flatbreads
2 x 125g (4½ oz) fresh mozzarella, well drained and sliced
leafy greens, store-bought tzatziki and lemon wedges, to serve

Heat half the oil in a large frying pan over medium–high heat.

Add the garlic and cook for 30 seconds. Add the beef and harissa and cook, stirring, for 5 minutes.
Add the remaining oil and carrot and cook for a further 4 minutes or until the beef is well browned.

Add the paprika, tomato paste, parsley, salt and pepper and cook for 1 minute. Remove from
the pan. Wipe the pan clean with absorbent kitchen paper and return to medium heat.

Divide the beef mixture and mozzarella between each flatbread, keeping it on one half. Fold over
to enclose. Brush both sides of the flatbread with oil and cook for 5 minutes or until charred
and crisp.

Serve with a leafy greens, tzatziki and lemon wedges. **SERVES 2**

*Cook's note: Change up the beef mince for lamb, chicken or pork.
If you don't have harissa paste, chilli paste is a good substitute.
Flatbreads, pita breads, tortillas and Lebanese breads all work well
for this dish.*

This simple pasta works overtime on flavour – *punchy garlic,* zesty lemon, *peppery rocket,* flakes of tuna and silky pasta are just so good together. And it's simple enough that you can grab the ingredients at the supermarket on your way home – *too easy!*

tuna, rocket and lemon pasta

400g (14 oz) dried spaghetti or linguine
2 tablespoons extra virgin olive oil
1 tablespoon shredded lemon rind
3 cloves garlic, sliced
1 teaspoon dried chilli flakes
sea salt and cracked black pepper
¼ cup (60ml/2 fl oz) lemon juice
½ cup (125ml/4 fl oz) pure (pouring) cream
400g (14 oz) can tuna in oil, drained and broken into pieces
150g (5½ oz) rocket (arugula) leaves
lemon wedges, to serve

Cook the pasta in a large saucepan of boiling salted water until al dente. Drain, reserving ½ cup (125ml/4 fl oz) of the pasta water and set aside.

Return the saucepan to medium heat. Add the oil, lemon rind, garlic, chilli, salt and pepper and cook for 1 minute or until the garlic is golden.

Add the pasta, lemon juice, cream and reserved pasta water and toss to combine. Add the tuna and rocket and fold to combine.

Divide between bowls and serve with lemon wedges. **SERVES 4**

Cook's note: I like the chunky texture of larger tuna flakes for this pasta. I buy tuna fillets or tuna in a jar so I know it's going to have big flakes, which adds a great texture to this simple pasta.

shortcuts on a *classic*

We all have our favourite *comfort-food dishes* that we go back to again and again. But often those *traditional recipes* take a lot of time and effort. These quick, clever *makeovers* reinvent my favourite classics in a *new, speedy way*. I've created new shortcut versions of the dishes you love, so you can enjoy these nostalgic classics *without the fuss!*

When I'm cooking the classics, I like to create shortcuts. I think of these recipes as super-clever new versions that deliver on time as well as taste. Get ready to enjoy some of your favourites, only in record time!

in this chapter

If you love everything about lasagne *except the time it takes to make it,* then this is for you. This is not a traditional recipe for lasagne – it's more for those wanting all the *comforting gooey yumminess* of lasagne but *in an instant.* Try it – you'll love it!

one-pan undone lasagne

2 tablespoons extra virgin olive oil
1 brown onion, finely chopped
3 cloves garlic, crushed
600g (1 lb 5 oz) beef mince
1 litre (34 fl oz) good-quality beef stock
3 x 400g (14 oz) cans crushed tomatoes
2 tablespoons chopped oregano leaves
sea salt and cracked black pepper
250g (9 oz) fresh lasagne sheets, cut into 5cm x 21cm (2 in x 8½ in) strips
¼ cup (5g/⅛ oz) chopped basil leaves, plus extra leaves to serve
mascarpone cheese topping
350g (12½ oz) mascarpone
1 cup (80g/2¾ oz) finely grated parmesan, plus extra to serve
1 x 125g (4½ oz) fresh mozzarella, drained and sliced

Heat a large deep ovenproof frying pan over medium–high heat.

Add the oil and onion and cook for 5 minutes or until soft and golden. Add the garlic and beef and cook for 6 minutes, stirring, until the beef is well browned. Add the stock, tomatoes, oregano, salt and pepper and bring to the boil.

Reduce the heat to medium and simmer for 35–40 minutes or until the mixture has reduced by roughly one-third. The mixture should still be quite saucy.

Add the lasagne sheets, a few at a time, and gently stir to combine. Cook, stirring occasionally, for 3 minutes or until the pasta softens. Remove from the heat and stir through the basil.

Preheat oven grill (broiler) to high.

To make the mascarpone cheese topping, combine the mascarpone, parmesan and pepper. Top the lasagne with small spoonfuls of mascarpone mixture and mozzarella. Grill for 10–12 minutes or until the lasagne is golden and bubbly.

Finish with extra basil and parmesan to serve. **SERVES 6**

Cook's note: If you have dried lasagne sheets, pop them into boiling water for 30 seconds or until pliable, drain and use as you would fresh sheets.

Once you've tried this *insanely easy* shortcut for silky mac and cheese, you'll never look back. I am kicking myself that I didn't develop this recipe years ago. This is one of *my sons' favourite* dishes so I could have saved hours, if not days, by now, while still getting the same *deliciously creamy and comforting results.*

easiest one-pot mac and cheese

1.5 litres (51 fl oz) milk
sea salt and cracked black pepper
300g (10½ oz) dried macaroni
4 egg yolks, lightly whisked
1½ cups (180g/6½ oz) coarsely grated cheddar cheese
1 cup (80g/2¾ oz) finely grated parmesan

Place the milk, salt and pepper in a large saucepan over medium–high heat and bring to a simmer.

Add the pasta and cook for 8–10 minutes or until al dente. Remove from the heat.

Add the egg yolks to the cooked pasta, stirring until the sauce has thickened. Add the cheddar and parmesan and stir until melted. Sprinkle with extra salt and pepper, if desired, and serve.
SERVES 4

Cook's tip: Change up the combination of cheeses to make your own version. Stir through baby spinach leaves or grated broccoli to add a hit of green goodness. Or add a little kick with a spoonful of dijon.

This is a *fresh, lighter take* on the traditional version of pasta alla vodka. It's the same sweet tomato sauce *spiked with a little vodka* but I've added some soft creaminess by using burrata. Just tear over the top for the most beautifully *perfect finish.*

summer tomato vodka spaghetti

400g (14 oz) dried spaghetti
2 tablespoons extra virgin olive oil
1 brown onion, finely chopped
⅓ cup (80g/2¾ oz) tomato paste (concentrated purée)
600g (1 lb 5 oz) cherry tomatoes, halved
sea salt and cracked black pepper
⅓ cup (80ml/2½ fl oz) vodka
2 burrata, well drained
finely grated parmesan, to serve

Cook the pasta in a large saucepan of boiling salted water until al dente. Drain and set aside, reserving ½ cup (125ml/4 fl oz) of the pasta water.

Heat a large deep frying pan over medium heat. Add the oil and onion and cook for 6–7 minutes or until golden and soft.

Add the tomato paste and cook for 30 seconds. Add the cherry tomato, salt and pepper and cook for 5 minutes or until softened. Add the vodka and cook for 1 minute.

Add the reserved pasta water and pasta and mix to combine.

Divide the pasta among bowls, tear the burrata over the top and sprinkle with parmesan to serve.
SERVES 4

Cook's note: This recipe is tastiest when tomatoes are ripe, juicy and in season (in the summer). You can also use 2 x 400g cans of cherry tomatoes instead of using fresh. Squash the whole canned cherry tomatoes a little so they break down slightly.

Taco night just got a whole lot *easier and tastier!* You can bake this pan of *crisp and delicious* tacos in no time, then pop in the middle of the table and top with whatever *freshness you love.*

chipotle chicken traybake tacos

8 x 20cm (8 in) flour tortillas
1 tablespoon extra virgin olive oil, plus extra for brushing
1 red onion, sliced
400g (14 oz) can cherry tomatoes
¼ cup (60g/2 oz) chipotle chillies in adobo sauce, chillies finely chopped and sauce reserved
1 tablespoon honey
3 x 180g (6½ oz) chicken breast fillets, thinly sliced
2 teaspoons smoked paprika
400g (14 oz) can black beans
sea salt and cracked black pepper
1½ cups (180g/6½ oz) grated manchego or cheddar cheese
chopped avocado, coriander (cilantro) leaves, finely sliced jalapeño and lime wedges, to serve

Preheat oven to 180°C (350°F). Brush a 21cm x 28cm (8¼ in x 11 in) baking dish with oil.

Brush both sides of the tortillas with oil and place them in the prepared dish. Arrange them together, side-by-side, to form rustic cup-like shapes.

To make the filling, heat a large frying pan over medium–high heat. Add the oil and onion and cook for 5 minutes or until soft. Add the cherry tomatoes, chipotle and reserved sauce and honey and cook for 5 minutes or until thickened.

Add the chicken and paprika and cook for 5 minutes or until the chicken is cooked through.

Remove from the heat and fold through the black beans, salt and pepper.

Spoon the mixture into tortillas, top with cheese and bake for 20 minutes or until the tortillas are golden and crisp.

Serve with avocado, coriander, jalapeño and lime wedges. **SERVES 4**

Cook's note: Spice things up by swapping the chicken with sliced spicy chorizo.

This is not the meatloaf I remember from my childhood! This is seriously well-flavoured, with a *crispy layer of maple bacon* that makes it an *absolute showstopper* for any dinner table, picnic spread, or layered into a crisp baguette for lunch.

apple, sage and maple bacon meatloaf

extra virgin olive oil, for brushing
2 cups (140g/5 oz) fresh breadcrumbs
⅓ cup (80ml/2½ fl oz) milk
sea salt and cracked black pepper
750g (1 lb 11 oz) pork mince
1 egg
1 cup (80g/2¾ oz) finely grated parmesan
2 tablespoons chopped oregano leaves
2 cloves garlic, crushed
1 tablespoon dijon mustard
14 bacon rashers, rind removed
1 apple, thinly sliced (about 10 slices)
6 sage sprigs
2 tablespoons pure maple syrup
rocket (arugula) leaves, to serve

Preheat oven to 180°C (350°F). Brush a 21cm x 28cm (8¼ in x 11 in) baking dish with oil.

Combine the breadcrumbs, milk, salt and pepper in a bowl and set aside for 10 minutes.

Add the pork, egg, parmesan, oregano, garlic and mustard and mix well for 3 minutes to combine.

Line the prepared dish with 12 bacon rashers, overlapping to cover the base and sides, allowing the excess to hang over the edges.

Press the pork mixture into the dish and fold excess bacon over the filling to enclose the mixture. Cover with remaining bacon. Top with apple slices and sage leaves and brush with 1 tablespoon of the maple syrup.

Cook for 30–35 minutes or until the meatloaf is cooked through.

Turn the oven grill (broiler) to high.

Drain any excess cooking liquid from the dish then brush top of the meatloaf with the remaining maple syrup.

Grill for 4 minutes or until golden. Serve with rocket. **SERVES 4-6**

This recipe is the best of two worlds – a *golden and cheesy cauliflower gratin* wrapped up in a crisp pastry shell. Best of all, you can mix and match with any ingredients you have at hand to create *your own signature dish.*

cauliflower cheese galette

1 cup (100g/3½ oz) grated gruyère
¾ cup (185g/6½ oz) mascarpone
¼ cup (20g/¾ oz) finely grated parmesan
1 egg yolk
cracked black pepper
400g (14 oz) store-bought ready rolled shortcrust pastry
700g (1 lb 9 oz) cauliflower, thinly sliced
30g (1 oz) unsalted butter, melted

Preheat oven to 200°C (400°F).

Combine the gruyère, mascarpone, parmesan, egg yolk and pepper.

Join the pastry sheets together to form a rough 30cm (1 ft/12 in) round, trimming if necessary.

Place the pastry on a baking tray lined with non-stick baking paper.

Spread the mascarpone mixture over the pastry, leaving a 2cm (¾ in) border.

Top with cauliflower and fold the excess pastry over to form an edge. Brush the pastry edges with butter and bake for 30–35 minutes or until golden and cauliflower is tender. **SERVES 4**

Cook's note: Take the base of this recipe (the pastry and the cheesy filling) and top with anything you like to make your own signature galette. Try sliced cooked potatoes and rosemary, thinly sliced celeriac or fennel. The possibilities are only limited by your creativity!

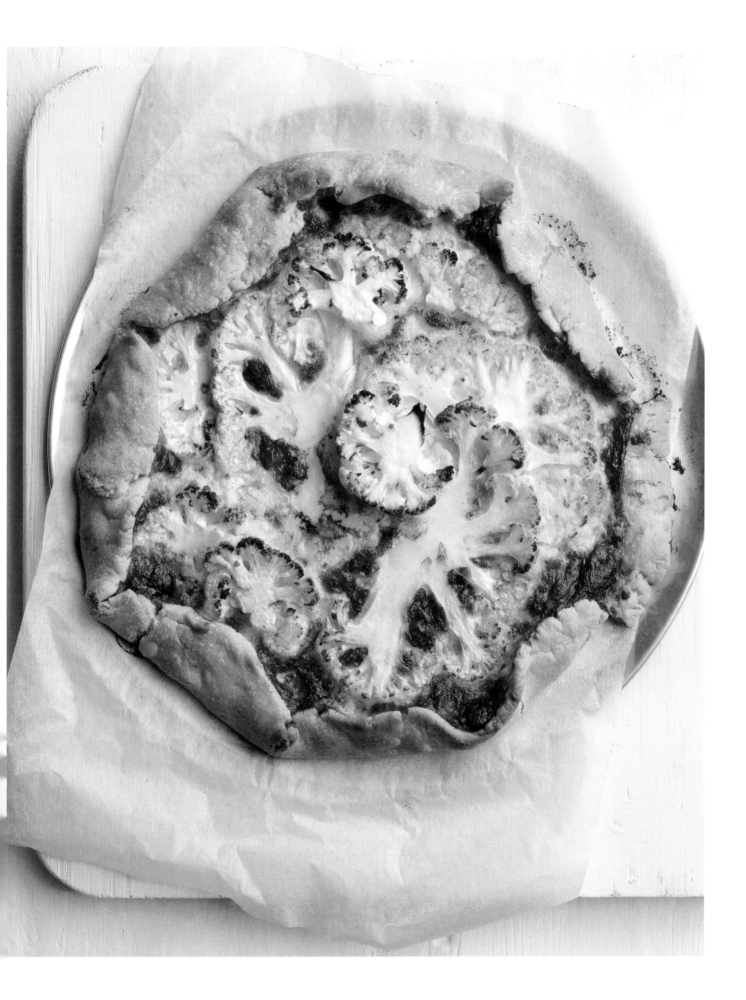

Pack *more flavour into your schnitzel* with a layer of olive tapenade and a crunchy parmesan crumb. Then it all goes under the grill to create the *crispiest golden crust* that makes this such an irresistible dinner. Plus, it's all ready in *less than 20 minutes!*

olive and parmesan-crusted chicken schnitzel

4 x 180g (6½ oz) chicken breast fillets, trimmed and halved lengthwise
⅓ cup (75g/2¾ oz) store-bought olive tapenade
4 cups (280g/10 oz) fresh sourdough breadcrumbs
1 cup (80g/2¾ oz) finely grated parmesan
¼ cup (5g/⅛ oz) torn oregano leaves
cracked black pepper
extra virgin olive oil, for drizzling
lemon wedges, rocket (arugula) leaves, sliced heirloom tomatoes and olives, to serve

Preheat oven grill (broiler) to high.

Place the chicken on a baking tray lined with non-stick baking paper. Spread each chicken fillet with olive tapenade.

Combine the breadcrumbs, parmesan, oregano and pepper. Top each chicken fillet with the breadcrumb mixture and press to coat.

Drizzle generously with oil, then grill for 10–12 minutes or until golden and cooked through.

Serve the schnitzels with lemon wedges and a salad of rocket, tomato and olives. **SERVES 4**

Cook's note: A delicious twist is to swap the olive tapenade for store-bought basil pesto.

This salmon pie has a *zesty lightness* from the lemon and crème fraîche in combination with the super-crisp layers of scrunched filo. You get all *the comfort of a traditional pie,* but it takes a fraction of the time and effort – so clever, so delicious.

creamy salmon and leek pie

60g (2 oz) unsalted butter, plus extra melted butter for brushing
1 tablespoon extra virgin olive oil, plus extra for brushing
2 leeks, trimmed and sliced
1 tablespoon plain (all-purpose) flour
⅓ cup (80ml/2½ fl oz) dry white wine or fish stock
600g (1 lb 5 oz) fillet sustainably caught salmon, skin removed, cut into 3cm (1¼ in) chunks
400g (14 oz) asparagus, trimmed and chopped into chunks
400g (14 oz) crème fraîche
¼ cup (12g/½ oz) chopped dill or tarragon leaves
3 teaspoons dijon mustard
2 teaspoons finely grated lemon rind
sea salt and cracked black pepper
12 filo pastry sheets
2 teaspoons sesame seeds
green salad, to serve

Preheat oven to 200°C (400°F).

Heat the butter and oil in a deep ovenproof frying pan over medium–high heat.

Add the leek and cover with a tight-fitting lid. Cook for 5 minutes, stirring occasionally, or until soft. Sift over the flour and cook, stirring, for 30 seconds.

Add the wine or stock and cook for 1 minute, stirring, or until reduced. Remove from the heat.

Add the salmon, asparagus, crème fraîche, dill or tarragon, mustard, lemon rind, salt and pepper and stir through.

Brush each sheet of filo pastry with oil and fold each sheet into quarters. Scrunch the sheets on top of the salmon mixture to cover. Brush with extra melted butter and sprinkle with sesame seeds.

Bake for 20 minutes or until the pastry is golden. Serve the pie with a crisp green salad. **SERVES 4**

Cook's note: If asparagus is not in season, you can also use 1 cup of frozen peas or finely chopped broccoli.

This genius 'one-pan pie' gives a *classic favourite* a new look. The *crisp parmesan–potato topping* is a delicious change-up to the traditional mash. So easy, so clever!

cheat's shepherd's pie

¼ cup (35g/1¼ oz) plain (all-purpose) flour
sea salt and cracked black pepper
1kg (2 lb 3 oz) boneless lamb shoulder, trimmed and cut into 2cm (¾ in) chunks
2 tablespoons extra virgin olive oil, plus extra for brushing
2 brown onions, cut into thin wedges
4 cloves garlic, crushed
2 carrots, finely chopped
2 stalks celery, finely chopped
400g (14 oz) can diced tomatoes
2 cups (500ml/17 fl oz) good-quality beef stock
2 tablespoons worcestershire sauce
1kg (2 lb 3 oz) potatoes, peeled and sliced into 5mm (¼ in) thick rounds
½ cup (40g/1½ oz) finely grated parmesan

Preheat oven to 220°C (425°F).

Combine the flour, salt and pepper in a large bowl. Add the lamb and toss to coat.

Heat half the oil in a large deep ovenproof frying pan over medium–high heat. In batches, add the lamb and cook for 4 minutes or until golden brown. Remove and set aside.

Add the remaining oil, onion, garlic, carrot and celery and cook for 8 minutes or until softened. Add the tomatoes, stock and worcestershire sauce and stir to combine.

Return the lamb to the pan and bring to a simmer. Cook for 20 minutes, then remove from the heat.

Top the lamb mixture with potato, brush with oil and sprinkle with salt.

Place on a baking tray and cook in the oven for 40 minutes. Sprinkle the potatoes with parmesan and cook for a further 10 minutes or until the lamb is tender and the potatoes are golden. **SERVES 4**

Cook's note: Change out the carrots and celery in this pie for chopped parsnip, celeriac, broccoli or pumpkin, or any veg combo you love.

honey...
I bought an
air fryer

My sons campaigned hard (and made me watch a lot of TikToks), until finally, in the name of work-related research, *I bought an air fryer!* I've loved experimenting with the dishes in this chapter to figure out if it *lives up to the hype.* My verdict? It's perfect for fast bites that thrive on *extra crunch* (like my new go-tos here). For bigger pieces of meat, I'll stick with my *trusty oven,* though.

I find that preheating the air fryer gives food a better crunch. These ideas are all quick, delicious and big on the crisp-and-golden factor. So tempting, so easy!

in this chapter

The trick of using *parmesan-sandwiched tortillas* to make a crispy 'pastry' shell is genius! So quick, simple, *and so delicious!*

cheat's pumpkin, sage and ricotta quiche

500g (1 lb 2 oz) butternut pumpkin, peeled, seeds removed and chopped into chunks
extra virgin olive oil, for drizzling
sea salt and cracked black pepper
2 x 30cm (12 in) flour tortillas
melted unsalted butter, for brushing
⅓ cup (25g/1 oz) finely grated parmesan
100g (3½ oz) feta, broken into large chunks
8 sage leaves
quiche filling
4 eggs, lightly whisked
⅔ cup (160ml/5½ fl oz) pure (pouring) cream
½ cup (40g/1½ oz) finely grated parmesan, extra

Preheat air fryer to 200°C (400°F) for 4 minutes. Reduce the heat to 180°C (350°F).

Add the pumpkin to the basket. Drizzle with oil and sprinkle with salt and pepper. Bake for 15 minutes or until just soft. Remove from the air fryer and set aside.

Line the air fryer basket with two pieces of non-stick baking paper, allowing them to overlap.

Brush both sides of the tortillas with melted butter. Sprinkle one tortilla with parmesan and top with the remaining tortilla. Place the sandwiched tortillas into the lined basket (see *cook's note*).

Bake for 5 minutes or until the tortilla case is lightly golden. Reduce the heat to 140°C (275°F).

To make the quiche filling, whisk together the egg, cream, extra parmesan, salt and pepper.

Pour the mixture into the tortilla case and top with the pumpkin, feta and sage leaves. Bake for 25–30 minutes or until just cooked but with a slight wobble in the centre. Stand for 10 minutes before serving. **SERVES 4**

Cook's note: This recipe needs an air fryer with a basket. Choose tortillas that are bigger than the base of your basket. Once you place the tortillas in, you want them to come a little way up the sides of the basket to hold the quiche filling.

My boys asked me for a *meatball sub* and this is what I made for them! Once their plates were completely empty, they asked, 'Are there seconds?' Looks like this one is going to be *on lunchtime repeat* for quite a while!

sweet chilli chicken meatball banh mi

700g (1 lb 9 oz) chicken mince
2 cups (140g/5 oz) fresh breadcrumbs
¼ cup (13g/½ oz) chopped coriander (cilantro) leaves
¼ cup (60ml/2 fl oz) sweet chilli sauce, plus extra to serve
2 tablespoons finely grated ginger
2 teaspoons finely grated lime rind
sea salt flakes
¾ cup (100g/3½ oz) sesame seeds, for rolling
extra virgin olive oil, for brushing
fresh baguettes, mayonnaise, sliced cucumber, sliced carrot, coriander (cilantro) leaves, sliced long red chilli and lime wedges, to serve

Combine the chicken, breadcrumbs, coriander, chilli sauce, ginger, lime rind and salt and mix well to combine.

Place the sesame seeds in a shallow bowl.

Shape the mixture into 12 meatballs and roll each meatball in the sesame seeds until coated.

Preheat air fryer to 200°C (400°F) for 4 minutes.

Brush the hot basket with oil. In batches, add the chicken meatballs to the basket and brush with extra oil. Cook for 8 minutes or until cooked through.

To assemble, spread the baguettes with mayonnaise. Top with cucumber, carrot, meatballs, coriander and chilli. Serve with a drizzle of extra sweet chilli and lime wedges. **SERVES 4**

Cook's note: To ensure your meatballs are light, fluffy and super easy to roll, be sure to mix them for at least 3 minutes to allow the protein in the chicken to bind all the ingredients together.

The *crispy crunch of fried chicken* is irresistible, but deep-frying uses a lot of oil. Enter this air-fried version. You get *all the satisfaction* but it's on the lighter side. *So yum!*

air fryer crispy buttermilk chicken

8 x 125g (4½ oz) chicken thigh fillets, trimmed
2 cups (500ml/17 fl oz) buttermilk
3 teaspoons Chinese five-spice
4 cups (240g/8½ oz) panko (Japanese) breadcrumbs
1½ teaspoons smoked paprika
2 teaspoons sea salt flakes
1 teaspoon cracked black pepper
spray oil, for cooking
slaw, potato chips and mayonnaise, to serve

Combine the chicken, buttermilk and five-spice and refrigerate for 30 minutes.

Preheat air fryer to 200°C (400°F) for 4 minutes.

Combine the breadcrumbs, paprika, salt and pepper in a shallow bowl.

Spray the hot basket with oil. In batches, drain the chicken from the buttermilk mixture and immediately press into the breadcrumb mixture for a thick and even coat.

Add the chicken to the basket and spray generously with extra oil. Cook for 8 minutes, turn over, spray with more oil and cook for a further 8 minutes or until crispy.

Serve with a simple slaw, potato chips and mayonnaise. **SERVES 4-6**

Cook's note: Spraying the chicken with oil before you cook it works a treat to evenly coat the chicken, resulting in a super-crisp, golden crumb. If you don't have any spray oil, be sure to oil the chicken well with a brush.

A *sweet, glistening marinade* pairs with flavour-packed pork, crisped to perfection in the air fryer, to create a super-simple dinner that *disappears in moments.*

sticky crispy pork belly

900g (2 lb) pork belly piece, skin removed, cut into 3½ cm (1¼ in) chunks
steamed rice, coriander (cilantro) leaves and blanched Asian greens (optional), to serve
sticky honey marinade
⅓ cup (80ml/2½ fl oz) hoisin sauce
¼ cup (60ml/2 fl oz) soy sauce
¼ cup (90g/3 oz) honey
2 tablespoons rice wine vinegar
1 tablespoon sesame oil
1 tablespoon finely grated ginger

To make the sticky honey marinade, combine the hoisin, soy sauce, honey, vinegar, sesame oil and ginger in a large bowl.

Add the pork and refrigerate for 1 hour or overnight. Remove the pork from the marinade, reserving the marinade. Set aside.

Preheat air fryer to 160°C (325°F) for 4 minutes.

Brush the hot basket with oil. Add the pork and brush with oil. Cook for 20 minutes, then turn and cook for a further 15 minutes or until golden and crispy.

Meanwhile, place the reserved marinade in a saucepan over medium heat and cook for 4 minutes or until thick and caramelised. Remove from the heat.

Add the pork to the marinade and toss until well coated. Transfer to a serving plate and serve with rice, coriander leaves and Asian greens, if desired. **SERVES 4**

Cook's note: Choose a cut of pork belly that is not too fatty as the fat won't render out in an air fryer like it does when slow—cooked in an oven.

These *mini mouth-tingling bites* are my absolute faves – *crunchy on the outside* with *pillowy soft tofu* on the inside. I could happily eat a bowl of these for movie night, or any night! Add a *tangle of noodles* and greens to create a satisfying meal.

crispy salt and pepper tofu

1¼ cups (160g/5½ oz) cornflour (cornstarch)
1 tablespoon finely crushed sichuan peppercorns
2 teaspoons Chinese five-spice
1 teaspoon chilli powder
½ teaspoon sea salt flakes
3 egg whites, whisked by hand to soft peaks
vegetable oil, for brushing
cooked udon noodles, blanched Asian greens, store-bought crispy chilli oil, shichimi togarashi and furikake, to serve
marinated tofu
700g (1 lb 9 oz) firm tofu, cut into large chunks
½ cup (125ml/4 fl oz) soy sauce
½ cup (125ml/4 fl oz) mirin (Japanese rice wine)
2 tablespoons caster (superfine) sugar

To make the marinated tofu, place the tofu in a flat container. Combine the soy sauce, mirin and sugar. Pour over the tofu to cover. Allow to marinate for 1 hour or overnight. Remove the tofu and discard the marinade.

Combine the cornflour, peppercorns, five-spice, chilli powder and salt.

Preheat air fryer to 200°C (400°F) for 4 minutes.

Brush the hot basket with oil. In batches, dip the tofu in egg white and press into the cornflour mixture.

Add the tofu to the basket and brush generously with extra oil. Cook the tofu for 5 minutes, turn, brush with more oil and cook for a further 5 minutes or until crispy.

To serve, divide the udon noodles and Asian greens between bowls. Top with the crispy salt and pepper tofu, crispy chilli oil, togarashi and furikake. **SERVES 4**

Cook's note: To get the full impact of the zingy numbing tingle that sichuan peppercorns give, always use freshly crushed peppercorns. Pre-ground peppercorns just don't give the same result.

If you love *big umami flavours,* you can spice things up with this vibrant bowl of *crisp marinated chicken* and *crunchy veg.* I prepare all the elements in advance so when it's time for dinner, all that's left to do is pop the *chicken in the air fryer* and serve!

spicy korean chicken rice bowls

6 x 125g (4½ oz) chicken thigh fillets, trimmed and cut into small chunks
3 egg whites, lightly whisked
1½ cups (245g/8½ oz) cornflour (cornstarch)
extra virgin olive oil, for brushing
4 cups (740g/1 lb 10 oz) cooked jasmine rice
4 cups (200g/7 oz) red cabbage, thinly sliced
2 green onions (scallions), thinly sliced
1⅓ cups (375g/13 oz) kimchi
store-bought crispy chilli oil and sesame seeds, to serve
spicy Korean-style marinade
¼ cup (60ml/2 fl oz) light soy sauce
¼ cup (75g/2¼ oz) gochujang (Korean chilli paste)
2 tablespoons rice wine vinegar
2 tablespoons honey
1 tablespoon sesame oil
4 cloves garlic, crushed
1 tablespoon finely grated ginger

To make the spicy Korean-style marinade, combine the soy sauce, gochujang, vinegar, honey, sesame oil, garlic and ginger.

Add the chicken and toss to coat. Refrigerate for 30 minutes. Remove the chicken and discard the marinade.

Preheat air fryer to 200°C (400°F) for 4 minutes.

Place the cornflour in a shallow bowl.

Brush the hot basket with oil. In batches, dip the chicken in the egg white and press both sides in the cornflour to coat.

Add the chicken to the hot basket and brush generously with oil. Cook for 3–4 minutes each side or until crisp, golden and cooked through.

Divide the rice between bowls. Top with cabbage, green onion, kimchi, chicken, crispy chilli oil and sesame seeds to serve. **SERVES 4**

When making *crispy rice* the traditional way, I'm often filled with panic that the rice will get stuck to the pan. But... hello air fryer and my new *perfect crispy rice method!* It's deliciously crunchy on one side, soft on the other, and best of all, no sticking!

crispy rice salad with lime and chilli chicken

3 cups (555g/1 lb 4 oz) cooked jasmine rice
2 tablespoons vegetable oil, for brushing
250g (9 oz) green beans, blanched and halved
2 cups (32g/1¼ oz) coriander (cilantro) leaves
2 cups (32g/1¼ oz) mint leaves
3 green onions (scallions), thinly sliced
lime and chilli chicken
6 Thai lime leaves, thinly sliced
2 teaspoons finely grated lime rind
¼ cup (60ml/2 fl oz) lime juice
¼ cup (60ml/2 fl oz) fish sauce
2 long green chillies, seeds removed and shredded
2 tablespoons firmly packed brown sugar
3 x 180g (6½ oz) cooked chicken breasts, shredded

Preheat air fryer to 200°C (400°F) for 4 minutes.

Place a piece of non-stick baking paper into the basket of the air fryer.

Add the rice and spread out to flatten. Brush the top with oil and cook for 30 minutes or until the top of the rice is golden and crisp. Break the crispy rice into chunks.

To make the lime and chilli chicken, combine the lime leaves, lime rind and juice, fish sauce, chilli and brown sugar. Add the chicken and toss to coat.

To assemble, combine the beans, coriander and mint and place on a platter. Add the chicken and drizzle with remaining dressing. Top with crispy rice and green onions to serve. **SERVES 4**

Cook's note: This dish is a great way to use up leftover cooked rice.

I can't get enough of these *crisp, no-fuss pies* with the tastiest creamy, cheesy filling. Swapping pastry for tortillas is *a genius game changer,* and the potential to switch up the flavours to suit you and your family (or what's in the fridge) is *even better.*

speedy spinach and ricotta pies

400g (14 oz) frozen spinach, thawed
2 cups (480g/1 lb 1 oz) fresh ricotta
1 egg, plus 2 extra eggs, lightly whisked, for brushing
¾ cup (60g/2 oz) finely grated parmesan
¼ cup (12g/½ oz) finely chopped dill leaves
2 teaspoons finely grated lemon rind
sea salt and cracked black pepper
4 x 20cm (8 in) flour tortillas
extra virgin olive oil, for brushing

Squeeze the excess liquid from spinach and finely chop.

Combine the spinach, ricotta, 1 egg, parmesan, dill, lemon rind, salt and pepper.

Divide the mixture between tortillas, placing the mixture in the centre.

Brush the edges with whisked egg, fold each of the tortillas in half and press edges to seal.

Preheat air fryer to 200°C (400°F) for 4 minutes. Reduce the heat to 180°C (350°F).

Brush the hot basket with oil. In batches, place the pies in the basket and brush one side with egg. Cook for 7 minutes each side or until golden and crispy. Sprinkle with salt to serve. **MAKES 4**

Cook's note: You can easily switch up the flavour combos here. Try cooked chicken mixed with sour cream and chives for an almost-instant chicken pie. Chunks of roasted pumpkin, semi sundried tomatoes with feta... let your imagination run wild!

Crispy French toast collides with a *gooey double-cheese ham toastie* in this indulgent recipe that hits the spot for breakfast, lunch, dinner... or *whenever it takes your fancy, really!*

french toast ham and cheese toastie

¼ cup (75g/2½ oz) whole-egg mayonnaise
2 teaspoons dijon mustard
4 thick sourdough slices
150g (5¼ oz) thinly sliced ham
100g (3½ oz) soft brie, sliced
1 cup (100g/3½ oz) grated gruyère
4 eggs, lightly whisked
¼ cup (60ml/2 fl oz) milk
sea salt flakes
60g (2 oz) unsalted butter, melted
4 small sage leaves

Combine the mayonnaise and mustard.

Spread the bread with the mustard mayonnaise. Top 2 of the slices with ham, brie and gruyère and sandwich with remaining bread.

Preheat air fryer to 180°C (350°F) for 4 minutes.

Whisk the egg, milk and salt to combine.

In batches, dip the sandwich in the egg mixture for 30 seconds–1 minute each side or until the bread has absorbed the egg mixture and is soft. Place the sandwich onto a small piece of non-stick baking paper and place in the hot basket. Drizzle with a little of the melted butter and cook for 8 minutes.

Flip the sandwich and top with 2 sage leaves that have been dipped in the egg mixture. Drizzle with a little of the melted butter and cook for a further 4 minutes or until golden and crisp.

Repeat with remaining ingredients to make the other sandwich. **SERVES 2**

Cook's note: Switch up the filling by replacing the ham with any sliced meat and adding any of your favourite types of cheese.

I wouldn't have believed it if I hadn't made this recipe myself. Can you really cook a cheeseburger patty in an air fryer and get *perfectly juicy* results? Absolutely yes – *I am completely sold.*

the ultimate air fryer cheeseburger

700g (1 lb 9 oz) beef mince
1 cup (60g/2 oz) panko (Japanese) breadcrumbs
⅓ cup (100g/3½ oz) store-bought caramelised onion relish or chutney
2 tablespoons dijon mustard
1 tablespoon tomato paste (concentrated purée)
sea salt and cracked black pepper
extra virgin olive oil, for brushing
8 thin cheese slices
4 burger buns, halved
whole-egg mayonnaise, butter lettuce, store-bought tomato chutney, sliced dill pickles and potato chips, to serve

To make the patties, combine the beef, breadcrumbs, relish, mustard, tomato paste, salt and pepper in a bowl and mix very well. Divide the mixture into 4 flat patties (around 12cm/4¾ in in diameter).

Preheat air fryer to 200°C (400°F) for 4 minutes.

Brush the hot basket with oil. In batches, cook the patties for 8 minutes or until browned and cooked through. Top each with 2 slices of cheese and cook for 1–2 minutes or until the cheese is melted.

To assemble, spread each of the burger buns with mayonnaise. Top with lettuce, patties and tomato chutney. Serve with dill pickles and potato chips. **SERVES 4**

Cook's note: You can swap the beef mince for chicken or pork, and add whatever toppings you like.

Technically this isn't a standalone dinner recipe, but these golden, crunchy and *seriously snackable chips* are great served alongside many of the dishes in this book. And I won't judge if you enjoy them *all by themselves,* either!

polenta chips with whipped goat's cheese

2 cups (500ml/17 fl oz) good-quality chicken stock
1 cup (250ml/8½ fl oz) milk
1 cup (170g/6 oz) instant polenta
sea salt and cracked black pepper
1 cup (80g/2¾ oz) finely grated parmesan
extra virgin olive oil, for brushing
whipped goat's cheese
100g (3½ oz) mascarpone
100g (3½ oz) soft goat's cheese
⅓ cup (80g/2¾ oz) plain thick Greek yoghurt

Line a 20cm (8 in) square cake tin with non-stick baking paper.

Place the stock and milk in a medium saucepan over high heat. Bring to the boil.

Gradually whisk in the polenta, reduce the heat to medium–low and cook, whisking continuously, for 6 minutes or until very thick.

Add the salt, pepper and parmesan and mix to combine. Spoon the mixture into the prepared tin, spread evenly and flatten. Refrigerate for 15–20 minutes or until cooled and firm.

Cut the polenta in half and slice into 2cm (¾ in)-thick chips.

Preheat air fryer to 200°C (400°F) for 4 minutes.

Brush the hot basket with oil. In batches, place the chips in the basket and brush the tops of the chips with oil. Cook for 5 minutes each side or until golden.

To make the whipped goat's cheese, whisk together the mascarpone, goat's cheese and yoghurt. Sprinkle with pepper and whisk until smooth.

Sprinkle the chips with salt and serve with the whipped goat's cheese. **SERVES 4 AS A SIDE**

Cook's note: You could add some herby flavour here by stirring chopped chives into the polenta mixture with the parmesan, or sprinkling over chopped rosemary before baking the polenta chips.

This is where the *air fryer gets bougie*. This is a clever salad – simple enough to dish up for a *light weeknight dinner* and fabulous enough to serve as a side *when you have friends over.*

charred sweet cabbage with whipped tahini dressing

¼ cup (60ml/2 fl oz) extra virgin olive oil, plus extra for drizzle
1½ tablespoons honey
1 tablespoon ras el hanout
sea salt flakes
2 baby sugarloaf cabbages, halved
½ cup (16g/½ oz) mint leaves
½ cup (24g/1 oz) flat-leaf (Italian) parsley leaves
½ cup (80g/2¾ oz) roughly chopped toasted almonds
½ cup (80g/2¾ oz) pomegranate seeds
pomegranate molasses, for drizzling
whipped tahini dressing
1 cup (280g/10 oz) hulled tahini
1 cup (250ml/8½ fl oz) cold water
¼ cup (60ml/2 fl oz) lemon juice

Combine the oil, honey, ras el hanout and salt in a large bowl. Spoon over the cut-side of the cabbage to coat.

Preheat air fryer to 200°C (400°F) for 4 minutes.

Brush the hot basket with oil. In batches, add the cabbage to the basket and cook for 15 minutes or until soft and charred.

While the cabbage is cooking, make the whipped tahini dressing. Place the tahini, water, lemon juice and salt in a blender and blend until light, thick and creamy.

To serve, divide the cabbage, mint, parsley, almond and pomegranate seeds between plates. Drizzle with pomegranate molasses and oil. Serve with whipped tahini dressing. **SERVES 4**

Cook's note: I use this whipped tahini dressing on everything! It's so simple yet so flavourful, and is perfect spooned over anything from salads to roasted vegetables or roasted chickpeas. Make double and keep in the fridge for up to 5 days!

This is the first dish that made me *fall in love* with my air fryer. My *go-to weeknight salad* is now so much quicker to make – crispy, golden and delicious roast cauliflower in just 20 minutes (this usually takes me an hour in the oven)! *Love!*

crispy tahini-cauliflower salad

¼ cup (60ml/2 fl oz) extra virgin olive oil, plus extra for brushing
1½ tablespoons lemon juice
sea salt and cracked black pepper
3 cups (490g/1 lb 1 oz) cooked quinoa
1 cup (52g/2 oz) roughly chopped flat-leaf (Italian) parsley leaves
1 cup (56g/2 oz) roughly chopped mint leaves
150g (5½ oz) feta, broken into chunks
lemon wedges, to serve
crispy tahini cauliflower
⅓ cup (90g/3 oz) hulled tahini
¼ cup (60ml/2 fl oz) apple cider vinegar
2 tablespoons honey
1 teaspoon smoked paprika
750g (1 lb 11 oz) cauliflower florets

To make the crispy tahini cauliflower, whisk the tahini, vinegar, honey, paprika and salt to combine. Add the cauliflower and toss to coat.

Preheat air fryer to 200°C (400°F) for 4 minutes. Reduce the heat to 180°C (350°F).

Brush the hot basket with oil. In batches, add the tahini cauliflower to the basket. Brush with oil and cook for 10 minutes. Turn the cauliflower and cook for a further 10 minutes or until golden and crisp.

To make the salad, whisk the oil, lemon juice, salt and pepper to combine. Add the quinoa, parsley, mint and feta and toss to coat.

To serve, divide the salad among plates and top with crispy tahini cauliflower. Serve with lemon wedges. **SERVES 4**

Cook's note: This crispy cauliflower also makes a great snack.
To spice things up a little, add some dried chilli flakes to the tahini mix and serve with some store-bought tzatziki for a cool and creamy side.

all in One

The *best dinners* are not only flavour-packed *people pleasers;* they're simple to prepare, leaving you less to wash up. These clever *one-pan* and *one-tray wonders* meet the brief: super satisfying all-in-one meals you can toss together with *minimal fuss,* saving you time but dialling up the deliciousness.

Your weeknight dinner repertoire is set for a shake-up! Put these clever ideas on repeat for super-simple dinners that give big returns on flavour with less fuss.

in this chapter

Level up the flavour on your chicken parma by baking it with layers of parmesan, *creamy mozzarella,* oregano and crispy prosciutto. The roast tomatoes and balsamic sauce make the *perfect finish.*

balsamic tomato chicken parma

¼ cup (60ml/2 fl oz) balsamic vinegar
1 tablespoon extra virgin olive oil, plus extra for drizzling
1 tablespoon firmly packed brown sugar
sea salt and cracked black pepper
600g (1 lb 5 oz) cherry tomatoes
4 x 180g (6½ oz) chicken breast fillets, trimmed
¾ cup (60g/2 oz) finely grated parmesan
2 x 125g (4½ oz) fresh mozzarella, well drained and sliced into 8 pieces
4 oregano sprigs
8 slices prosciutto

Preheat oven to 200°C (400°F).

Combine the balsamic vinegar, oil, sugar, salt and pepper.

Place the tomatoes on a baking tray lined with non-stick baking paper and pour over the balsamic mixture. Bake for 15 minutes.

Place the chicken on a board and sprinkle with parmesan and pepper. Top each with 2 slices of the mozzarella and a sprig of oregano. Place 2 slices of prosciutto on top of each, folding them underneath the chicken to enclose.

Place the chicken on top of the tomatoes and drizzle with oil. Cook for 12–15 minutes or until the chicken is golden and cooked through. **SERVES 4**

Cook's note: I've used cherry tomatoes on the vine here – however you can use any cherry tomatoes you like. Roma tomatoes cut into quarters also work well. The key is to buy whatever tomato is ripe and sweet.

This dish, also known as assassin's pasta, is packed with *flavour and crunch,* and is one of my *favourite ways to eat spaghetti.* Cooking it in a flavoured tomato broth gives a deep richness – that *addictive crispiness* reminds me of the edges of a lasagne. Yum!

caramelised tomato spaghetti

¼ cup (60ml/2 fl oz) extra virgin olive oil
2 cloves garlic, finely sliced
½ teaspoon dried chilli flakes, plus extra to serve
2 tablespoons capers, rinsed
4 anchovies, chopped
400g (14 oz) dried spaghetti
finely grated parmesan, to serve
tomato broth
1 litre (34 fl oz) boiling water
1½ cups (375ml/12½ fl oz) tomato passata (purée)
2 tablespoons tomato paste (concentrated purée)
sea salt and cracked black pepper

To make the tomato broth, combine the water, passata, tomato paste, salt and pepper in a large jug or saucepan.

Place the oil, garlic, chilli, capers and anchovies in a large deep frying pan over medium–high heat and cook for 2 minutes or until fragrant.

Add the pasta and 1 cup (250ml/8½ fl oz) of the tomato broth and gently move the spaghetti to prevent it from sticking together.

When the pasta has absorbed the broth, pour in another 1 cup (250ml/8½ fl oz) of tomato broth.

Cook, stirring occasionally, allowing the pasta to absorb the stock and to start to caramelise.

Repeat this process until the pasta is cooked al dente and some of the pasta has a caramelised, crisp crust. Turn off the heat and allow the pasta to stand for a minute or two and the pasta will lift from the pan. Sprinkle with parmesan and extra chilli to serve. **SERVES 4**

Cook's note: If you're not into anchovies, just leave them out. Replace them with a good pinch of salt or top your pasta with some finely chopped olives for a little salty zing.

The thing I love most about this *flavourful, fall-apart* chicken? You can use it as the base for so many different dinners. Serve it with tacos, pasta, rice or beans; no matter what, *it will shine!*

simple chicken and chorizo ragu

1 tablespoon extra virgin olive oil
2 brown onions, finely chopped
2 chorizo (220g/8 oz), sliced
4 x 125g (4½ oz) chicken thigh fillets, trimmed
1 cup (250ml/8½ fl oz) good-quality chicken stock
2 x 400g (14 oz) cans cherry tomatoes
1 tablespoon tomato paste (concentrated purée)
1 teaspoon smoked paprika
sea salt and cracked black pepper
flour tortillas, sliced avocado, sliced long green chillies, coriander (cilantro) leaves
   and lime wedges, to serve

Heat a large frying pan over medium–high heat.

Add the oil, onion and chorizo and cook for 6 minutes or until golden.

Add the chicken, stock, tomatoes, tomato paste and paprika and bring to a simmer.

Reduce the heat to medium and cover with a tight-fitting lid. Simmer for 25 minutes. Remove the lid and simmer for a further 5 minutes or until the sauce has thickened.

Sprinkle with salt and pepper to taste and stir to combine.

Serve with tortillas, avocado, green chilli, coriander and lime wedges. **SERVES 4**

Cook's note: Switch out the canned cherry tomatoes for canned chopped tomatoes, if you like. This recipe makes a great freezer dinner base, so double the recipe and freeze half for later.

Not only is baking your curry *incredibly easy,* but it means you get those delicious caramelised edges on the chicken and added *richness* from the slowly reduced sauce. Try it – *you'll love it!*

creamy coconut curry chicken bake

¼ cup (75g/2¾ oz) store-bought Thai red curry paste, plus 1 tablespoon extra
1 tablespoon finely grated ginger
1 stalk lemongrass, trimmed and white part only, finely grated
1 cup (250ml/8½ fl oz) good-quality chicken stock
400ml (13½ fl oz) coconut cream
6 x 180g (6½ oz) chicken thigh cutlets, skin-on and bone-in
600g (1 lb 5 oz) baby potatoes
650g (1 lb 7 oz) pumpkin, skin-on and cut into large chunks
extra virgin olive oil, for drizzling
coriander (cilantro) sprigs and thinly sliced green onions (scallions), to serve

Preheat oven to 220°C (425°F).

Combine the curry paste, ginger, lemongrass, stock and coconut cream. Place the chicken and extra curry paste in a separate bowl and mix until the chicken is well coated. Set aside to marinate.

Place the potatoes and pumpkin in a deep-sided baking dish and pour over the red curry mixture.

Bake the potatoes and pumpkin for 20 minutes or until the potatoes are beginning to brown. Add the chicken to the dish, skin-side up, and drizzle with a little oil. Bake for a further 25–30 minutes or until the chicken is golden and cooked through.

Serve with coriander and green onion. **SERVES 4**

Cook's note: You can mix up the veg in this curry – try sweet potato, big wedges of fennel or eggplant, or some halved parsnips or carrots. Whatever you love or whatever you have to hand, this curry recipe will adapt with the same delicious results.

Crowd-favourites pasta and meatballs get a *creamy, cheesy makeover*. My secret to the *most flavourful meatballs?* It's the sneaky piece of bocconcini tucked inside each one.

creamy parmesan chicken meatball pasta bake

2 tablespoons extra virgin olive oil
1 leek, finely sliced
2⅔ cups (660ml/22½ fl oz) good-quality chicken stock
1½ cups (375ml/12½ fl oz) pure (pouring) cream
2⅔ cups (410g/14½ oz) baby tube pasta or macaroni
120g (4½ oz) baby spinach leaves
basil leaves, to serve
parmesan chicken meatballs
1½ cups (105g/3½ oz) fresh breadcrumbs
⅓ cup (80ml/2½ fl oz) milk
700g (1 lb 9 oz) chicken mince
1½ cups (120g/4½ oz) finely grated parmesan, plus extra to serve
1½ tablespoons chopped oregano
2 egg yolks
1 clove garlic, crushed
sea salt and cracked black pepper
12 baby bocconcini

Preheat oven to 180°C (350°F).

To make the meatballs, combine the breadcrumbs and milk in a large bowl and soak for 5 minutes. Add the chicken, parmesan, oregano, egg, garlic, salt and pepper and mix well to combine. Shape ⅓-cupfuls of the chicken mixture into 12 flat patties. Press a bocconcini into the centre of each patty then fold over the mixture to enclose and form a meatball shape.

Heat a large deep ovenproof frying pan over medium heat. Add half the oil and the meatballs and cook for 3 minutes each side or until golden. Remove from the pan and set aside.

Return the pan to a medium heat. Add the remaining oil and the leek, and cook, stirring, for 6 minutes or until soft and golden. Add the stock and cream and bring to a simmer then add the pasta and stir to combine. Return the meatballs to the pan and cover with a tight-fitting lid. Place in the oven and bake for 20–25 minutes or until the pasta is al dente and the meatballs are cooked through.

Add the baby spinach and stir through until the leaves have wilted.

To serve, sprinkle with extra parmesan and basil leaves. **SERVES 4**

The winning combination of *tangy lemon and yoghurt* not only gives a boost of flavour, but it's also the key to perfectly tenderised chicken. The addition of *dill and capers* adds even more punch.

lemon, yoghurt and dill grilled chicken

8 x 125g (4½ oz) chicken thigh fillets, trimmed and cut into chunks
2 lemons, thinly sliced
mint leaves, flat-leaf (Italian) parsley leaves, pomegranate seeds, lemon wedges and
    extra plain thick Greek yoghurt, to serve
lemon, yoghurt and dill marinade
1 cup (250g/9 oz) plain thick Greek yoghurt
¼ cup (12g/½ oz) chopped dill leaves
2 teaspoons finely grated lemon rind
1 tablespoon rinsed and finely chopped capers
2 tablespoons lemon juice
1 tablespoon extra virgin olive oil, plus extra for drizzling
sea salt and cracked black pepper

To make the lemon, yoghurt and dill marinade, combine the yoghurt, dill, lemon rind, capers, lemon juice, oil, salt and pepper in a large bowl. Add the chicken and mix to combine. Set aside to marinate for 30 minutes.

Preheat oven grill (broiler) to high. Line a large baking tray with non-stick baking paper and top with lemon slices.

Thread the marinated chicken onto 12 metal skewers and place on top of the lemons. Drizzle with oil and grill for 12 minutes or until cooked through.

Serve the skewers with mint, parsley, pomegranate seeds, lemon wedges and yoghurt. **SERVES 4-6**

Cook's note: To ensure the chicken cooks quickly and evenly, I prefer to use metal skewers.

Inspired by two of my *favourite Japanese dishes,* this simple one-tray recipe is loaded with textures and bold flavours. It is low on effort but I promise you *seriously satisfying* returns.

crispy miso and sesame chicken on sticky soy eggplant

4 x 180g (6½ oz) chicken breast fillets, trimmed and halved lengthways
¼ cup (55g/2 oz) white miso paste
1½ tablespoons honey, extra
¾ cup (100g/3½ oz) sesame seeds
vegetable oil, for drizzling
thinly sliced green onion (scallions) and coriander (cilantro) leaves, to serve
sticky soy eggplant
⅓ cup (80ml/2½ fl oz) mirin (Japanese rice wine)
¼ cup (60ml/2 fl oz) soy sauce
¼ cup (90g/3 oz) honey
1 tablespoon sesame oil
850g (1 lb 14 oz) eggplant (aubergine) (about 3), cut lengthways into thin slices

Preheat oven to 220°C (425°F).

To make the sticky soy eggplant, heat a saucepan over medium heat.

Add the mirin, soy sauce, honey and sesame oil and bring to a rapid simmer. Cook for 5 minutes or until the mixture has reduced by half. Remove from the heat.

Place the eggplant on a large baking tray lined with non-stick baking paper. Brush the eggplant with half the soy mixture and bake for 15 minutes or until the eggplant is starting to caramelise.

While the eggplant is cooking, prepare the chicken. Combine the miso and extra honey.

Place the sesame seeds in a shallow bowl.

Spread a thin layer of the miso mixture on one side of each chicken fillet and press into the sesame seeds to coat.

Preheat oven grill (broiler) to high.

Place the chicken on top of the eggplant and drizzle with vegetable oil. Grill the chicken and eggplant for 6–8 minutes or until the sesame seeds are golden and the chicken is cooked through.

Spoon over remaining soy mixture and serve with green onions and coriander. **SERVES 4**

This is the roast chicken that overdelivers – you must try it! Baking the chicken over *simmering caramelised onions* flavours the meat while keeping it super juicy, and the mustard and honey gives the chicken a *glorious golden glaze.* Amazing!

honey mustard and caramelised onion baked chicken

⅓ cup (95g/3¼ oz) dijon mustard
1½ tablespoons honey
12 small sage leaves, extra
1.8kg (4 lb) whole chicken, back bone removed, halved
sea salt and cracked black pepper
caramelised onions
1kg (2 lb 3 oz) brown onions (about 6 onions), sliced
2 tablespoons extra virgin olive oil
1 cup (250ml/8½ fl oz) good-quality chicken stock
2 sprigs sage

Preheat oven to 200°C (400°F).

To make the caramelised onions, place the onion and oil in a large deep ovenproof frying pan and cook over medium heat for 10–12 minutes or until soft and starting to brown. Add the stock and sage and cook until the stock is simmering.

Combine the mustard and honey and spread over the chicken. Top with the extra sage leaves.

Place the chicken onto the caramelised onions, sprinkle with salt and pepper and place in the oven. Bake for 40–45 minutes or until the chicken is cooked through.

Cut the chicken into pieces and serve with the onions and pan sauce. **SERVES 4**

Cook's note: The cook time here will depend on the size of your chicken. Check smaller chickens for readiness at 35 minutes. Larger chickens may take up to 55 minutes to cook through.

If you're in need of a *warming and comforting* dish that has huge yum factor, this easy bake is your new go-to. *Soft creamy risoni with crunchy, cheesy edges...* talk about a dream combo!

pork and fennel pasta bake

1 tablespoon extra virgin olive oil
2 brown onions, chopped
1 teaspoon fennel seeds, lightly crushed
500g (1 lb 2 oz) pork mince
1 litre (34 fl oz) good-quality chicken stock
½ cup (125ml/4 fl oz) milk
300g (10½ oz) dried risoni
2 teaspoons finely grated lemon rind
sea salt and cracked black pepper
1 cup (250ml/8½ fl oz) pure (pouring) cream
1 x 125g (4½ oz) fresh mozzarella, drained and sliced
11 sage leaves
¾ cup (60g/2 oz) finely grated parmesan
rocket (arugula) leaves or crisp green salad, to serve

Heat a large deep ovenproof frying pan over medium–high heat.

Add the oil, onion and fennel seeds and cook for 5 minutes or until the onion is soft and golden. Add the pork and cook for 6 minutes or until brown, stirring and breaking up any large lumps.

Pour in the stock and milk and bring to the boil. Reduce the heat to medium–low.

Add the risoni, lemon rind, salt and pepper. Cover and cook, simmering, for 12 minutes or until the risoni is al dente.

Preheat oven grill (broiler) to high.

Stir through the cream and top the mixture with mozzarella, sage and parmesan. Grill for 10 minutes or until golden. Serve with rocket leaves or a crisp green salad. **SERVES 4**

Cook's note: You can easily swap the pork mince for chicken mince in this recipe and it's just as delicious. For my fussy eaters, I leave out the fennel seeds – easy!

This *warming pasta bake* pulls rank as one of the best of the best. Creamy, lemony pasta with *crisp, caramelised cubes* of haloumi – it delivers *pure delight* with every bite.

crispy haloumi and lemon risoni bake

1 tablespoon extra virgin olive oil, plus extra for drizzling
2 leeks, sliced
1½ cups (300g/10½ oz) dried risoni
2 teaspoons finely grated lemon rind
3½ cups (875ml/29½ fl oz) good-quality chicken stock
1 cup (250ml/8½ fl oz) pure (pouring) cream
2½ cups (90g/3 oz) firmly packed shredded kale leaves (about 2–3 stalks)
sea salt flakes
380g (13½ oz) haloumi, cut into chunks
1 tablespoon thyme leaves
½ teaspoon cracked black pepper
1 lemon, thinly sliced

Heat a large deep ovenproof frying pan over medium–high heat.

Add the oil and leek and cook for 6 minutes or until soft and golden.

Add the risoni, lemon rind, stock and cream and bring to a simmer. Simmer, stirring occasionally, for 9 minutes or until the risoni is just soft. Add the kale and salt and stir to combine.

Preheat oven grill (broiler) to high.

While the risoni is cooking, combine the haloumi, thyme and pepper.

Top the risoni with sliced lemon and the haloumi mixture and drizzle with extra oil. Transfer to the oven and grill for 10–12 minutes or until the haloumi is golden and crispy. **SERVES 4**

Cook's note: If you prefer, you can switch up the kale for baby spinach leaves and change thyme for oregano. I also like to drizzle a little honey on the haloumi before it bakes to add an extra dose of sweetly caramelised crunch.

One of the simplest *bursting-with-flavour* fish dishes you will make. The spice of the chorizo, sweet tomatoes and the *creaminess* of the beans is a *fantastic combo.* Try any sustainable, firm thick fish fillet – salmon, barramundi or ocean trout all work perfectly.

tomato and chorizo braised fish

1 tablespoon extra virgin olive oil
2 chorizo (220g/8 oz), sliced
600g (1 lb 5 oz) cherry tomatoes, halved
½ cup (125ml/4 fl oz) good-quality chicken stock
sea salt and cracked black pepper
400g (14 oz) can butter (lima) beans
4 x 150g (5½ oz) fillets sustainably caught firm white fish, skin removed
finely grated lemon rind, flat-leaf (Italian) parsley leaves and dried chilli flakes (optional),
   to serve

Heat a large deep frying pan over medium heat. Add the oil and chorizo and cook, stirring occasionally, for 5 minutes or until the chorizo is golden and crisp.

Add the tomato, stock, salt and pepper and simmer for 6 minutes. Add the beans and stir to combine.

Place the fish on top of the tomato mixture and cover with a tight-fitting lid. Cook for 6–8 minutes or until the fish is cooked to your liking.

Sprinkle with lemon rind, parsley and chilli to serve. **SERVES 4**

Cook's note: You can buy chorizo that is spicy or mild so choose the one that suits your tastes. If you want to replace the fresh cherry tomatoes with canned, increase the simmer time of the tomatoes by an extra 10 minutes before adding the fish so you have a nice rich sauce.

This *all-round winner* is often a star player at my take on taco night. It's a dish that has a little bit of everything – it's a little smoky, a little sweet, with a *kick of chilli* to finish. Perfect!

caramelised pork and chilli pineapple tacos

30g (1 oz) unsalted butter
2 tablespoons extra virgin olive oil
800g (1 lb 12 oz) fresh pineapple, skin and core removed, cut lengthways into quarters
6 long red chillies, halved and seeds removed
1 tablespoon smoked paprika
1 teaspoon chilli powder
sea salt and cracked black pepper
2 x 450g (1 lb) pork fillets, trimmed and cut in half
⅓ cup (80ml/2½ fl oz) apple cider or apple juice
2 tablespoons pure maple syrup
12 x 15cm (6 in) flour tortillas, warmed
2 avocados, deseeded and sliced
1 red onion, thinly sliced into rings
2 cups (32g/1¼ oz) small coriander (cilantro) sprigs
lime wedges, to serve

Heat a large ovenproof frying pan over medium–high heat. Add the butter and half the oil and cook until the butter has melted.

Add the pineapple and red chilli and cook for 3 minutes each side or until charred. Remove from the pan and set aside. Wipe the pan clean with absorbent kitchen paper.

Combine the paprika, chilli powder, salt and pepper and sprinkle over the pork to coat.

Return the pan to medium–high heat. Add the remaining oil and the pork and cook for 3 minutes, turning occasionally, until browned.

Add the apple cider or apple juice and maple to the pan. Cover the pan with a tight-fitting lid. Reduce the heat to medium-low and cook for 8–10 minutes or until the pork is just cooked through. Remove the pork from the pan, leaving the sauce in the pan, and set aside.

Return the pan to a medium heat and cook the sauce for 2 minutes or until reduced and thickened.

To serve, thinly slice the pork and pineapple and place on tortillas. Top with the chilli, avocado, onion, coriander and lime wedges. Spoon over a little of the pan sauce and serve. **SERVES 4**

This is one of those insanely easy recipes that makes you look like you are *totally winning at life*. It's easy enough to throw together for a weeknight but I'd be equally happy bringing this tart out when *entertaining friends*.

zucchini and leek tart

480g (1 lb 1 oz) store-bought ready rolled shortcrust pastry
350g (12½ oz) mascarpone
4 egg yolks
¾ cup (60g/2¼ oz) finely grated parmesan
1 tablespoon thyme leaves
450g (1 lb) zucchini (courgette) (about 2–3), thinly sliced into rounds
1 leek, trimmed and cut into thin strips
40g (1½ oz) unsalted butter, melted
sea salt and cracked black pepper
rocket (arugula) leaves or crisp leafy salad, to serve

Preheat oven to 220°C (425°F).

Join the pastry sheets together to form a rough 24cm x 35cm (9½ in x 13¾ in) rectangle, trimming if necessary.

Place the pastry on a baking tray lined with non-stick baking paper.

Combine the mascarpone, egg, parmesan and thyme. Spread the mixture over the pastry, leaving a 2.5cm (1 in) border.

Top with zucchini and leek and fold the edges of the pastry in to make a border.

Brush the zucchini and leek with butter and sprinkle with salt and pepper.

Bake for 30 minutes or until the pastry is golden, the zucchini is soft and the leeks are deep golden brown.

Serve with rocket leaves or a crisp leafy salad. **SERVES 4**

Cook's note: You can make a large tart like I have here or four individual tarts – just follow the same process of folding over the edges of the pastry to enclose the filling.

flavour
starters

Unlock the *power of your pantry* to deliver amazing dinners with ease. These dishes are created using a few key *not-so-secret ingredients* that are the ultimate flavour bombs, here to light up your cooking repertoire. Keep them on hand at all times, and fresh, delicious, satisfying meals will always be *within your reach.*

Keeping your kitchen well-stocked with versatile, flavour-packed ingredients is a huge help when it comes to solving the daily dinner problem! Think harissa, gochujang and frozen peas, to name a few.

in this chapter

This recipe will *blow your mind!* It's *super zingy and zippy* from the lemons while the parmesan and pine nuts add a decadent creaminess. Throw in the *pop of freshness* from the basil, and I could eat this on *high rotation* forever.

spaghetti with lemon pesto

400g (14 oz) dried spaghetti
lemon pesto
2 lemons
⅓ cup (80ml/2½ fl oz) lemon juice
¾ cup (80g/2¾ oz) pine nuts, toasted
½ cup (125ml/4 fl oz) good-quality extra virgin olive oil
1 clove garlic, chopped
1¼ cups (100g/3½ oz) finely grated parmesan, plus extra to serve
⅓ cup (8g/¼ oz) basil leaves, plus extra to serve
sea salt and cracked black pepper, plus extra to serve

Cook the pasta in a large saucepan of boiling salted water until al dente. Drain, reserving ½ cup (125ml/4 fl oz) of the pasta water and return the pasta to the pan.

While the pasta is cooking, make the lemon pesto. Wash the lemons under very hot water, then dry. Using a vegetable peeler, peel the lemons, ensuring to peel away the yellow part only and not the white pith. You should have about 35g (1¼ oz) lemon peel.

Place the lemon peel, lemon juice, pine nuts, oil and garlic into a food processor and process until finely chopped. Add the parmesan, basil, salt and pepper and process until you have a smooth paste.

Add the lemon pesto and enough of the reserved pasta water to the pasta to make a saucy consistency. Toss to coat.

Divide between bowls and top with extra parmesan and extra basil to serve. **SERVES 4**

Cook's note: When peeling your lemons, it is essential to only use the yellow peel. Any white pith will give your pesto a bitter taste. If you do not have a food processor, you can also use a handheld stick blender.

This winning dish heroes *two flavour starters* that work perfectly together. The miso adds a salty roundness to the salmon while the wasabi adds a *subtle kick* to the creamy peas. Keep both on hand and this delicious balancing act will *win you over every time.*

smashed wasabi peas with miso-buttered salmon

60g (2 oz) unsalted butter, extra
1 tablespoon extra virgin olive oil, extra
1½ tablespoons white miso paste
1½ tablespoons lemon juice
4 x 150g (5½ oz) fillets sustainably caught salmon, skin removed
shiso leaves (optional) and shredded nori, to serve
smashed wasabi peas
60g (2 oz) unsalted butter
1 tablespoon extra virgin olive oil
1 tablespoon wasabi paste or store-bought grated horseradish
500g (1 lb 2 oz) frozen peas
⅓ cup (18g/¾ oz) chopped mint leaves

To make the smashed wasabi peas, heat the butter and oil in a large frying pan over medium heat. Add the wasabi or horseradish and cook for 10 seconds or until fragrant.

Add the peas and cook for 3 minutes or until heated through. Using a fork, lightly mash half the peas. Add the mint and stir to combine. Remove from the pan and set aside. Wipe the pan clean.

To make the miso-buttered salmon, return the pan to a medium heat. Add the extra butter and extra oil and cook until the butter has melted.

Add the miso and lemon juice and stir to combine. Add the salmon and cook for 3 minutes, each side, or until cooked to your liking.

To serve, divide the smashed wasabi peas between plates and top with the miso buttered salmon. Sprinkle with shiso leaves, if desired, and nori and serve. **SERVES 4**

Cook's note: Use frozen peas rather than frozen baby peas, as the larger peas make a creamier mash.

This super-quick, tasty twist on tabouli is made with lentils. Add *smoky spiced lamb* and *cool yet spicy* harissa yoghurt, and you have the *perfect balance* of flavours and textures.

spiced lamb and lentil tabouli with harissa yoghurt

500g (1 lb 2 oz) boneless lamb loin, trimmed
2 teaspoons smoked paprika
2 teaspoons sumac
sea salt and cracked black pepper
lentil tabouli
400g (14 oz) can brown lentils, rinsed and drained
250g (9 oz) cherry tomatoes, sliced
1 cup (24g/1 oz) flat-leaf (Italian) parsley leaves
1 cup (16g/½ oz) mint leaves
2 green onions (scallions), thinly sliced
2 tablespoons extra virgin olive oil, plus extra for brushing
2 tablespoons lemon juice
harissa yoghurt
1 cup (250g/9 oz) plain thick Greek yoghurt
1½ tablespoons harissa paste

To prepare the lamb, brush both sides with oil.

Combine the paprika, sumac, salt and pepper and sprinkle all over the lamb.

Heat a frying pan over medium–high heat. Cook the lamb for 2–3 minutes each side or until cooked to your liking. Remove from the pan, cover and set aside.

To make the lentil tabouli, combine the lentils, tomato, parsley, mint and green onion.

Combine the oil, lemon juice, salt and pepper and pour over the lentil mixture. Toss to combine.

To make the harissa yoghurt, place the yoghurt in a bowl, top with harissa and swirl to combine.

To serve, slice the lamb and divide between serving plates. Serve with the lentil tabouli and spoonfuls of harissa yoghurt. **SERVES 4**

Cook's note: Swap the lamb loin for a piece of boneless lamb leg or lamb rump. You could also use a chicken breast, pork fillet or a piece of beef steak. This recipe and its flavours are super flexible.

Honey and gochujang provide the perfect balance of sweetness and spice in this winning dish. With soft slippery noodles and *juicy, seared prawns,* dinner just got a *whole lot better.*

gochujang noodles with sesame prawns

1 tablespoon sesame oil
1 tablespoon vegetable oil
4 cloves garlic, sliced
6 green onions (scallions), sliced, plus extra, thinly sliced, to serve
500g (1 lb 2 oz) Asian greens or broccolini, trimmed and chopped
¼ cup (75g/2¾ oz) gochujang (Korean chilli paste)
¼ cup (90g/3 oz) honey
600g (1 lb 5 oz) fresh egg noodles
sesame prawns
400g (14 oz) raw (green) prawns, peeled, deveined and tails intact
¼ cup (90g/3 oz) honey, extra
1½ tablespoons gochujang (Korean chilli paste), extra
1½ tablespoons sesame seeds
1 tablespoon sesame oil, extra

Heat a large frying pan or wok over high heat. Add the sesame oil, vegetable oil, garlic and green onion and cook for 1 minute or until fragrant. Add the Asian greens or broccolini and cook for 2–3 minutes or until softened.

Add the gochujang, honey and noodles and mix to combine. Cook for 3 minutes or until the noodles are cooked. Remove from the pan and divide between serving bowls.

To make the sesame prawns, heat a large non-stick frying pan over medium heat. Add the extra honey, extra gochujang, sesame seeds and extra sesame oil and cook for 1 minute or until mixture is thick and sticky. Add the prawns and cook, stirring, for 1–2 minutes or until cooked through.

Top the noodles with the sesame prawns. Sprinkle with extra green onions and serve. **SERVES 4**

Cook's note: You could easily swap the prawns for chopped chicken breast or thigh, and use steamed rice instead of noodles.

This burger has taken some *flavourful twists and turns!* The spice from the green curry paste and the sriracha in the juicy patty matched with gingery apple slaw, all sandwiched in a *soft bun,* is a *delight for the taste buds.*

thai-inspired pork burger with ginger apple slaw

600g (1 lb 5 oz) pork mince
½ cup (35g/1¼ oz) panko (Japanese) breadcrumbs
¼ cup (26g/1 oz) chopped coriander (cilantro) leaves
2 tablespoons Thai green curry paste
1 tablespoon finely chopped pickled ginger
1 tablespoon honey
1 tablespoon sriracha hot chilli sauce
1 tablespoon extra virgin olive oil
4 burger buns, halved
mayonnaise and lime wedges, to serve
ginger apple slaw
1 apple, core removed and shredded
2 cups (90g/3 oz) shredded cabbage
½ cup (8g/¼ oz) coriander (cilantro) leaves, extra
2 tablespoons chopped pickled ginger, extra
2 tablespoons pickled ginger liquid (from the pickled ginger jar)

To make the patties, place the pork, breadcrumbs, coriander, curry paste, ginger, honey and sriracha in a bowl and mix well to combine. Divide the mixture into 4 patties.

Heat a large non-stick frying pan or barbecue over medium heat. Add the oil and patties and cook for 4 minutes each side or until cooked through.

While the patties are cooking, make the ginger apple slaw. Combine the apple, cabbage, coriander, extra pickled ginger and pickled ginger liquid.

To assemble, spread one side of the burger buns with mayonnaise, top with the ginger apple slaw and the patties. Serve with lime wedges. **SERVES 4**

Cook's note: There are so many easy swaps for this recipe so you can make it your own. Swap pork mince for chicken, and firm pear can step in for the apple. Green curry paste could be swapped for red.

If you haven't tried cooking mushrooms this way, you're missing out. These *flavoursome, almost meaty, crisps* are nothing like the soft buttered mushrooms you know – these are *next level.*

miso cauliflower soup with crispy caramelised mushrooms

750g (1 lb 11 oz) cauliflower florets
450g (1 lb) potatoes (about 2), peeled and finely chopped (I like dutch cream)
1 litre (34 fl oz) good-quality chicken stock
2 tablespoons white miso paste
1 cup (250ml/8½ fl oz) pure (pouring) cream
tarragon leaves, to serve
extra virgin olive oil, for drizzling
crispy caramelised mushrooms
300g (10½ oz) fresh oyster and shiitake mushrooms, cut into 1cm (½ in) slices
20g (¾ oz) unsalted butter, melted
1 tablespoon white wine vinegar
2 teaspoons caster (superfine) sugar
2 teaspoons thyme leaves
sea salt and cracked black pepper

Preheat oven to 220°C (425°F).

To make the crispy caramelised mushrooms, combine the mushroom, butter, vinegar, sugar, thyme, salt and pepper.

Spread evenly on a baking tray lined with non-stick baking paper. Top with another sheet of non-stick baking paper and another baking tray to help keep the mushrooms flat while baking. Bake for 20 minutes, then turn the mushrooms over, replace the tray and cook for a further 20 minutes or until crispy and caramelised.

While the mushrooms are baking, make the soup. Place the cauliflower, potato, stock and miso in a saucepan over medium–low heat and bring to a simmer. Cover with a tight-fitting lid and cook for 30 minutes or until the potato and cauliflower are tender.

Add the cream and stir to combine. Using a handheld stick blender, blend until smooth. Divide the soup between bowls and top with tarragon, mushrooms, extra pepper and a drizzle of oil. SERVES 4

Cook's note: When baking the crispy caramelised mushrooms, you'll need two medium trays of the same size. The second tray is used to weigh down the mushrooms while they cook to make them crispy.

My fresh take on fish tacos takes *jalapeño-spiked fish cakes,* adds a punchy herby salsa and wraps it all up in soft lettuce cups. It's the *flavours of a seaside summer evening* in one tasty dish.

jalapeño fish cakes

3 coriander (cilantro) roots, chopped
½ cup (26g/1 oz) chopped coriander (cilantro) leaves, extra
¼ cup (45g/1½ oz) chopped pickled jalapeño, seeds removed, extra
2 teaspoons finely grated lime rind
800g (1 lb 12 oz) fillet sustainably caught firm white fish, skin removed and chopped
1 egg white
sea salt flakes
2 tablespoons vegetable oil
butter lettuce leaves, extra coriander (cilantro) sprigs and lime wedges, to serve
jalapeño salsa
¼ cup (45g/1½ oz) chopped pickled jalapeños
¼ cup (13g/½ oz) chopped coriander (cilantro) leaves
¼ cup (14g/½ oz) chopped mint leaves
¼ red onion, finely chopped
2 tablespoons lime juice

To make the jalapeño salsa, combine the pickled jalapeños, coriander, mint, onion and lime juice. Set aside.

Place the coriander root and extra leaves, extra pickled jalapeños and lime rind in a blender and blend until finely chopped. Add the fish, egg white and salt and pulse until finely chopped and the mixture comes together. Shape ¼-cupfuls of the mixture into patties.

Heat a large non-stick frying pan over medium–high heat. In batches, add a tablespoon of oil and patties and cook for 3 minutes each side or until golden and cooked through.

To serve, top the lettuce leaves with the jalapeño salsa, fish cakes, extra coriander sprigs and lime wedges. **SERVES 4**

Cook's note: I have used snapper fillets for this recipe, however you can use any firm white fish you like. Drain the jalapeño from the pickling liquid before chopping.

Gochujang not only adds heat to these *succulent ribs,* it also adds a *deep savoury sweetness* that's a step ahead of the flavour you get from ordinary chilli paste. The results are *oh-so addictive,* sticky ribs that my team now request on repeat for our lunches.

spicy korean-style ribs

1.9kg (4 lb 7 oz) American pork ribs, cut into doubles
spicy caramelised Korean-style marinade
⅔ cup (200g/7 oz) gochujang (Korean chilli paste)
½ cup (120g/4½ oz) firmly packed brown sugar
¼ cup (60ml/2 fl oz) mirin (Japanese rice wine)
¼ cup (60ml/2 fl oz) soy sauce
8 cloves garlic, crushed
2 tablespoons finely grated ginger
1 tablespoon sesame oil

Preheat oven to 140°C (275°F).

To make the spicy caramelised Korean-style marinade, combine the gochujang, sugar, mirin, soy sauce, garlic, ginger and sesame oil in a large bowl.

Dip the ribs in the marinade, one at a time, and place, meat-side down, on a baking tray lined with non-stick baking paper.

Pour over the remaining marinade and bake for 45 minutes. Turn the ribs over and baste with the pan sauce. Bake for a further 45 minutes.

Increase oven to 200°C (400°F) and cook for a further 10 minutes or until caramelised. **SERVES 4**

Cook's note: I like to use double ribs for this recipe as there is more surface area to caramelise to yummy golden levels, while keeping the insides tender and juicy.

Brining chicken is a must! And when you have the brine already made for you – I'm using the *liquid from my olive jar* here – why wouldn't you make the most of it to add a touch of extra flavour and succulence? *Super juicy, super easy!*

grilled olive-brined chicken with squashed tomato salad

½ cup (125ml/4 fl oz) olive brine (see *cook's note*)
2 tablespoons lemon juice
2 tablespoons oregano leaves
1 teaspoon sea salt flakes
4 x 180g (6½ oz) chicken breast fillets, trimmed and halved lengthways
squashed tomato salad
600g (1 lb 5 oz) heirloom cherry tomatoes
1 cup (20g/¾ oz) basil leaves
2 teaspoons finely grated lemon rind
2 tablespoons extra virgin olive oil, plus extra for brushing
sea salt and cracked black pepper
½ cup (80g/2¾ oz) pitted green sicilian olives, sliced

Place the olive brine, lemon juice, oregano and salt in a non-reactive container (see *cook's note*) and mix to combine. Add the chicken, cover and refrigerate for 15 minutes, then turn and marinate for a further 15 minutes. Remove the chicken from the brine and pat dry using absorbent kitchen paper. Discard the brine liquid.

Preheat char-grill pan to high. Brush the chicken with oil and grill for 3–4 minutes each side or until cooked through.

To make the squashed tomato salad, place the tomatoes, basil, lemon rind, oil, salt and pepper in a bowl and lightly squash with a fork or potato masher. Add the olive and mix to combine.

Divide the salad between plates and top with the chicken to serve. **SERVES 4**

Cook's note: When shopping for this recipe, buy green sicilian olives in brine. You'll need the olive brine to marinate the chicken breasts – when you do this, use a non-reactive container made from glass, plastic or stainless-steel.

This is the easiest *throw-together dinner* that's big on flavour and low on fuss. I like to place everything on a board in the middle of the table, so everyone can *build their own* plate.

lentil and lamb patties with parsley and feta salad

500g (1 lb 2 oz) lamb mince
400g (14 oz) can lentils, rinsed and drained
1 egg
3 teaspoons ras el hanout
2 teaspoons finely grated lemon rind
2 tablespoons chopped dill leaves
sea salt and cracked black pepper
extra virgin olive oil, for cooking and drizzling
pita bread and store-bought hummus, to serve
parsley and feta salad
2 lebanese cucumbers, sliced
1½ cups (36g/1¼ oz) flat-leaf (Italian) parsley leaves
200g (7 oz) feta, broken into chunks
¼ cup (40g/1½ oz) pine nuts, toasted
red wine vinegar, for drizzling

To make the lamb patties, place the lamb, lentils, egg, ras el hanout, lemon rind, dill, salt and pepper in a bowl and mix well to combine. Shape ¼-cupfuls of the mixture into patties.

Heat a non-stick frying pan over medium–high heat. In batches, add oil and patties and cook for 3 minutes each side or until golden and cooked through.

To make the parsley and feta salad, combine the cucumber, parsley, feta and pine nuts. Drizzle with red wine vinegar and oil and toss to combine.

Divide the lentil and lamb patties between plates and serve with parsley and feta salad, pita bread and hummus. **SERVES 4**

Cook's note: You can easily serve this recipe as part of a large grazing platter – just add extra flatbreads and more store-bought or homemade dips such as tzatziki, baba ghanoush or garlic dip.

With layers of *hard-working flavours,* from punchy harissa to buttery garlic, *zingy orange rind* and creamy fish, this rice dish is a showstopper from start to finish, and is simple enough to prepare for a *winning weeknight dinner.*

herbed fish and harissa pilaf

40g (1½ oz) unsalted butter
1 tablespoon extra virgin olive oil
1 brown onion, sliced
3 cloves garlic, crushed
1½ cups (300g/10½ oz) basmati rice, washed
1½ tablespoons harissa paste
sea salt and cracked black pepper
3 cups (750ml/25½ fl oz) good-quality chicken stock
1 teaspoon finely grated orange rind
2 tablespoons extra virgin olive oil
2 tablespoons finely chopped coriander (cilantro) leaves
2 tablespoons finely chopped dill leaves
4 x 150g (5½ oz) fillets sustainably caught cod, skin removed
harissa yoghurt (see *recipe* p128), toasted slivered almonds, extra coriander (cilantro) leaves
  and lemon wedges, to serve

Heat a large ovenproof frying pan over medium heat. Add the butter and oil and cook until melted.

Add the onion and cook, stirring, for 5 minutes or until soft. Add the garlic and cook for 30 seconds. Add the rice, harissa, salt and pepper and cook for 1 minute. Add the stock and orange rind and bring to the boil. Cover with a tight-fitting lid. Reduce heat to medium–low and cook for 10 minutes.

Preheat oven to 220°C (425°F).

Combine the oil, coriander, dill, salt and pepper in a large bowl. Add the fish and toss to coat.

Remove the lid from the frying pan. Add the fish and top with remaining coriander mix. Bake in the oven for 10 minutes or until the rice is golden and crisp and the fish is cooked.

Serve the fish and rice with harissa yoghurt, almonds, extra coriander and lemon wedges. **SERVES 4**

Cook's note: I often make this dish with different types of fish, from salmon to barramundi. They all work well with the spices and herbs.

When you need a vegetarian dish that will *knock your socks off,* I present this *exceptionally good curry.* It's a colourful playground of flavour and texture, from the nutty lentils and chickpeas to the soft, spicy eggplant and the *creamy paneer.*

baked lentil, eggplant and paneer curry

⅓ cup (80ml/2½ fl oz) extra virgin olive oil, extra

2 tablespoons harissa paste

650g (1 lb 7 oz) chopped eggplant (aubergine) (about 2)

350g (12½ oz) paneer, chopped

¼ cup (13g/1 oz) chopped coriander (cilantro) leaves, plus extra leaves to serve

plain thick Greek yoghurt, to serve

lentil curry

1 tablespoon extra virgin olive oil

2 brown onions, cut into thin wedges

2 tablespoons finely grated ginger

2 long red chillies, sliced, plus extra to serve

1 tablespoon ground cumin

1½ cups (300g/10½ oz) dried red lentils, rinsed

400g (14 oz) can chickpeas, drained and rinsed

400ml (13½ fl oz) can coconut milk

1½ cups (375ml/12½ fl oz) good-quality vegetable or chicken stock

sea salt and cracked black pepper

Preheat oven to 220°C (425°F).

To make the lentil curry, heat a large deep ovenproof frying pan over medium–high heat. Add the oil and onion and cook for 5 minutes or until soft. Add the ginger, chilli and cumin and cook for 30 seconds or until fragrant. Add the lentils, chickpeas, coconut milk, stock, salt and pepper and stir to combine. Remove from the heat.

Place ¼ cup (60ml/2 fl oz) of the extra oil and harissa in a large bowl. Add the eggplant and toss to coat. Place the eggplant on top of the lentil curry and bake in the oven for 20 minutes or until the lentils are just soft.

Combine the paneer, coriander, remaining oil and salt and toss to coat. Top the eggplant with the paneer and bake for a further 15 minutes or until the eggplant and lentils are cooked and the paneer is golden. Serve with extra chilli, extra coriander and yoghurt. **SERVES 4**

Cook's note: This is also delicious served with the harissa yoghurt – see recipe p128.

set and *forget*

A little chopping, a little mixing and *you're on your way!* These set-and-forget wonders combine *big flavours and clever cuts* that simmer away on the stovetop or in the oven, leaving you to *shine like a star.* I promise *maximum impact* for minimal effort. It's a *recipe for success!*

Turn on the oven and turn down the stress, I say! All these recipes require just a little prep with some hard-working flavours, then your oven or stovetop will do the rest of the heavy lifting.

in this chapter

I'll share with you the simple secret to this *next-level roast lamb...* the punchy flavours are rolled up neatly inside so they infuse the meat as it gently roasts. The *crispy lemon potatoes* are a game changer, too – it's rare that I serve a roast without them!

slow-cooked mint and mustard lamb with lemon potatoes

1.1kg (2 lb 7 oz) boneless lamb leg, shank remaining and trimmed
2 cloves garlic, crushed
1 tablespoon dijon mustard
⅓ cup (18g/¾ oz) chopped mint leaves
1 tablespoon chopped rosemary leaves
cracked black pepper
lemon potatoes
1.4kg (3 lb 1 oz) potatoes (about 8), peeled and cut in half
1 lemon, thinly sliced
2 tablespoons extra virgin olive oil
2 teaspoons sea salt flakes, plus extra for sprinkling
8 sprigs oregano

Preheat oven to 200°C (400°F).

To make the lemon potatoes, place the potato and lemon in a deep-sided roasting pan. Drizzle with oil, salt and oregano and toss to combine. Set aside.

Spread the meat-side of the lamb with garlic and mustard and sprinkle with mint, rosemary, extra salt and pepper. Roll to enclose the filling and tie with kitchen string to secure.

Place the lamb on top of the potatoes and roast for 50 minutes–1 hour or until the lamb is cooked to medium or to your liking. Remove the lamb from the dish and cover.

Increase oven temperature to 220°C (425°F). Return the potatoes to the oven and roast for 10–15 minutes or until golden and crisp. Slice the lamb and serve with the lemon potatoes. You could also add steamed greens to serve if you wish. **SERVES 4**

Cook's note: If you have a bone-in leg, remove the main bone by starting on the underside or less meaty side and making a cut all the way to the shank. Work your knife around the bone, until you can remove it. You can also ask your butcher to do this for you.

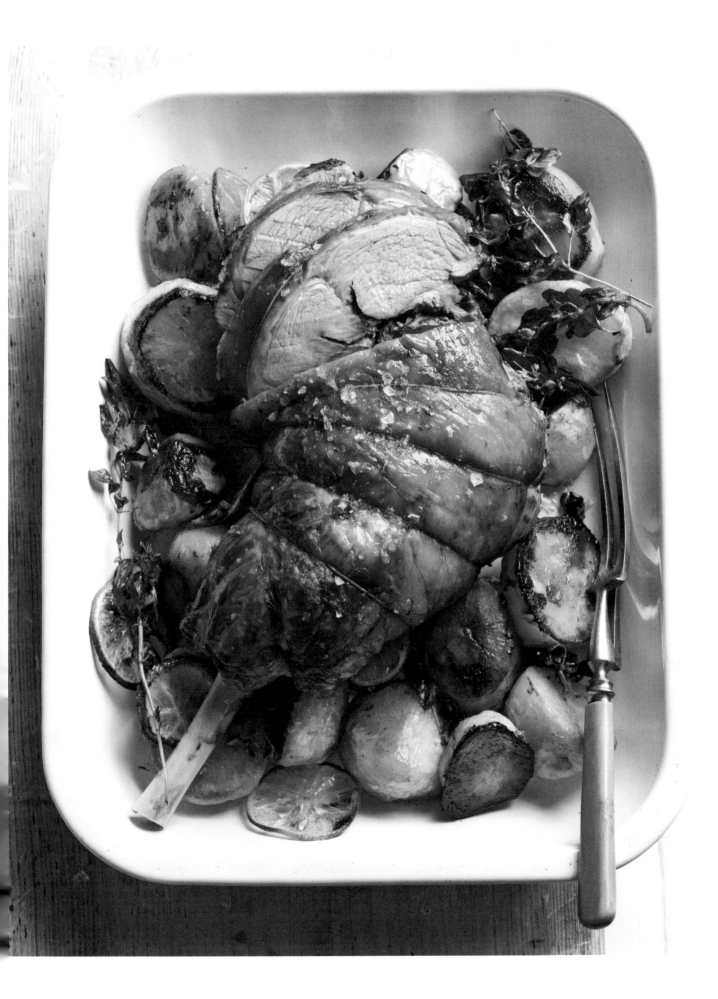

It's your favourite cheesy pasta with its *signature peppery kick* but revamped with a new look. This creamy set-and-forget risotto takes the *dreamy cheese–and–pepper combo* to delicious heights – and all you have to do is simmer, stir and bake!

cacio e pepe baked risotto

3½ cups (875ml/29½ fl oz) good-quality chicken stock
1 cup (250ml/8½ fl oz) pure (pouring) cream
1 tablespoon extra virgin olive oil
60g (2 oz) unsalted butter
1½ cups (300g/10½ oz) arborio or carnaroli rice
1½ teaspoons coarsely cracked black pepper, plus extra to serve
1 cup (80g/2¾ oz) finely grated parmesan or pecorino, plus extra to serve

Preheat oven to 180°C (350°F).

Place the stock and cream in a saucepan over medium–low heat. Bring to a simmer.

Heat a large deep ovenproof frying pan or flameproof roasting pan over medium heat. Add the oil, butter and rice and cook, stirring, for 2 minutes.

Add the stock mixture to the rice and stir to combine. Cover with a tight-fitting lid or aluminium foil and bake in the oven for 20 minutes. Allow to stand, covered, for 5 minutes. Remove the lid.

Add the pepper and parmesan or pecorino and stir for 5 minutes or until the risotto is creamy.

Serve with extra pepper and parmesan. This risotto is great served with a simple peppery rocket salad. **SERVES 4**

Cook's note: Take care not to overcook this risotto. It's a baked risotto that starts to thicken and become super creamy as you stir it at the end of the baking time – be patient, I assure you it will be perfect.

Golden, succulent roast chicken with *crunchy garlic bread* – need I say more? Just a little prep goes a long way here, and the toasts and vegetables act as a bed for the butterflied chicken as it cooks, soaking up all the *garlicky, buttery goodness.*

roast chicken with garlic sourdough toasts

2 leeks, trimmed and halved lengthways
185g (6½ oz) unsalted butter, softened
4 cloves garlic, crushed
1 teaspoon table salt
cracked black pepper
4 large thick sourdough slices
6 sprigs sage
6 sprigs thyme
8 unpeeled cloves garlic, extra
1 lemon, cut into wedges
1.5kg (3 lb 5 oz) whole chicken, butterflied and flattened
extra virgin olive oil, for drizzling

Preheat oven to 140°C (325°F).

Place the leeks in the base of a deep-sided roasting pan lined with non-stick baking paper.

Combine the butter, garlic, table salt and pepper. Spread half the butter mixture over the sourdough slices.

Place the sourdough slices, butter-side up, on the leeks and top with sage and thyme. Add the extra unpeeled garlic and lemon to the dish.

Using a small spoon, spread the remaining butter mixture under the skin of the breast and thigh of the chicken.

Place the chicken, breast-side up, on top of the bread and drizzle with oil. Bake for 1 hour 15 minutes or until the chicken is cooked. Serve the chicken with the soft leeks, crispy garlic bread and a green salad or simple slaw, if desired. **SERVES 4**

Cook's note: To butterfly the chicken, use sharp kitchen scissors to cut closely along each side of the backbone. Remove and discard the backbone. Turn the chicken, breast-side up, and press down firmly on the breastbone to flatten the chicken.

This is one of my *favourite ways* to cook pork. Braising the shoulder in milk gives a *lovely soft and mellow flavour* and the most divine juicy tenderness. Sage, leek and lemon are the perfect partners to *offset the richness* of the meat.

milk-braised pork shoulder with sage and leek

2kg (4 lb 6 oz) boneless pork shoulder, skin removed and trimmed of excess fat
⅓ cup (15g/½ oz) chopped sage leaves, plus 3 sprigs extra
1 tablespoon thyme leaves, plus 3 sprigs extra
sea salt and cracked black pepper
1 tablespoon extra virgin olive oil
2 leeks, trimmed and cut into quarters
4 strips lemon peel
3 bay leaves
1 litre (34 fl oz) milk
2 tablespoons unsalted butter, melted

Preheat oven to 180°C (350°F).

Sprinkle the meat-side of the pork with sage, thyme, salt and pepper. Roll to enclose the filling and tie with kitchen string to secure.

Heat oil in a large ovenproof saucepan or pot over high heat. Add the pork and cook for 5 minutes on each side or until browned. Remove the pork from the pan and set aside.

Add the extra sage sprigs, extra thyme sprigs, leek, lemon peel and bay leaves to the saucepan. Return the pork to the saucepan. Add the milk and cover with a tight-fitting lid.

Roast in the oven for 2 hours 40 minutes, turning the pork halfway.

Increase oven temperature to 200°C (400°F). Remove the lid and brush the pork with melted butter. Roast for a further 10 minutes or until golden. Remove the pork from the pan and set aside. Remove the sage, thyme, lemon peel and bay leaves and discard.

Using a handheld stick blender, carefully blend the hot milk and leeks until smooth.

Remove the kitchen string from the pork and slice. Serve with the leek sauce and roast vegetables. **SERVES 4**

Cook's note: Choose a pot that is small enough so, when you add the milk, it comes halfway up the sides of the pork. You want to ensure you have enough milk to poach the meat so it doesn't dry out.

With just a *simple combination* of a few ingredients, this lamb (literally!) shines. The pomegranate molasses, with its intense tang, is the *stand-out performer* here – it caramelises the lamb and lends a sensational colour and sweetness. *It's so easy!*

slow-cooked pomegranate-glazed lamb shoulder

3 brown onions, sliced into rounds
6–8 sprigs oregano
1.5kg (3 lb 5 oz) bone-in lamb shoulder, trimmed of excess fat
½ cup (125ml/4 fl oz) pomegranate molasses
3 cups (750ml/25½ fl oz) good-quality chicken stock
2 tablespoons lemon juice
1 tablespoon caster (superfine) sugar
1 teaspoon fennel seeds, lightly crushed
sea salt and cracked black pepper

Preheat oven to 160°C (325°F).

Place the onion and oregano in the base of a deep-sided roasting pan. Add the lamb, skin-side down.

Combine the pomegranate molasses, stock, lemon juice, sugar and fennel seeds and pour over the lamb. Sprinkle with salt and pepper.

Cover the pan tightly with non-stick baking paper and aluminium foil to create a tight seal. Roast for 2 hours.

Remove the cover and carefully turn the lamb over. Cover tightly again and roast for a further 1 hour or until the lamb is very tender.

Increase oven temperature to 180°C (350°F).

Remove the cover and discard. Roast the lamb for a further 30 minutes or until the lamb has a deep golden crust. This is delicious served with flatbreads and a tabouli or a tomato salad.
SERVES 4

Cook's note: Pomegranate molasses can be tricky to find but it's worth seeking out as it really makes a difference here. It's available in some supermarkets but can also be found in specialty grocers.

Say hello to your new *must-have pork recipe!* The rich depth of flavour that comes from the sauce – combined with the *tender, succulent meat* and the simple 'prep, set and forget' method – makes this an *essential addition to your dinner rotation.*

sticky soy and miso pork shoulder

12 slices ginger
2 star anise
6 cloves garlic, peeled and bruised
¼ cup (60ml/2 fl oz) soy sauce
¾ cup (180ml/6 fl oz) mirin (Japanese rice wine)
1 tablespoon sesame oil
3 cups (750ml/25½ fl oz) good-quality chicken stock
2 tablespoons white miso paste
¼ cup (60g/2 oz) firmly packed brown sugar
6 green onions (scallions), trimmed and cut into thirds, plus extra, sliced, to serve
1.5kg (3 lb 5 oz) boneless pork shoulder, trimmed of excess fat
cooked ramen noodles and blanched Asian greens, to serve

Preheat oven to 180°C (350°F).

Place the ginger, star anise, garlic, soy sauce, mirin, sesame oil, stock, miso and sugar in a medium deep-sided roasting pan or shallow casserole dish. Stir until the miso and sugar have dissolved.

Add the green onion and pork shoulder, skin-side up. Cover the pan tightly with non-stick baking paper and aluminium foil to create a tight seal. Roast for 2 hours.

Remove the cover and carefully turn the pork over so it is skin-side down. Cover tightly again and roast for a further 1 hour.

Increase oven temperature to 220°C (425°F).

Remove the cover and discard. Carefully turn the pork shoulder over so it is skin-side up. Roast for 15 minutes or until caramelised and crisp. Remove the pork from the sauce and slice. Skim the excess fat from the sauce and strain.

Serve the pork with ramen noodles, Asian greens, extra green onion and the sauce. **SERVES 4**

Cook's note: I also cooked this recipe using beef brisket instead of pork and it was sensational. You could also use chicken pieces – reduce cooking time to just an hour before uncovering and caramelising the meat. You'll be amazed at the results.

There's brisket, then there's this *tender, rich brisket* working overtime as it simmers away in a *herby, garlicky* balsamic sauce. Topping the brisket with onions is a neat little trick – they slowly caramelise into *the most perfect crust.* It's a genius move!

balsamic and sweet onion beef brisket

8 unpeeled cloves garlic
12 sprigs oregano
2 cups (500ml/17 fl oz) good-quality beef stock
¾ cup (180ml/6 fl oz) balsamic vinegar
¼ cup (60g/2 oz) firmly packed brown sugar, plus 1 tablespoon extra
1.5kg (3 lb 5 oz) beef brisket, trimmed of excess fat
sea salt and cracked black pepper
2 brown onions, sliced into rounds
1 tablespoon extra virgin olive oil

Heat a large ovenproof saucepan over medium heat. Add the garlic, oregano, stock, balsamic and sugar and stir until the sugar has dissolved.

Add the brisket, sprinkle with salt and pepper and bring to a simmer.

Combine the onion, oil, extra sugar, salt and pepper and arrange on top of the brisket.

Cover with a tight-fitting lid or non-stick baking paper and aluminium foil. Reduce the heat to low and simmer for 3 hours 30 minutes.

Preheat oven to 220°C (425°F).

Remove the lid and transfer the pan to the oven. Cook for 20 minutes or until the onion is caramelised and golden brown. Serve the brisket sliced or shredded. This is delicious served with roast vegetables, mashed potatoes or soft polenta with spoonfuls of the pan sauce. **SERVES 4**

Cook's note: The right-sized saucepan for this dish will depend on the shape and size of your brisket. When you first start cooking the brisket, ensure the liquid comes three-quarters up the side of the meat. This ensures it will be well-flavoured and won't dry out.

Who can resist *crisp, juicy pork belly?* Golden crunch on the outside, soft and tender meat on the inside... it's just all too delicious. Baking with *pears and juniper* adds sweetness and will infuse your home with *the most incredible aroma.*

crispy pork belly with pears and sage

1 tablespoon sea salt flakes
1.2kg (2 lb 10 oz) boneless pork belly, skin scored at 5cm (2 in) intervals
1 tablespoon extra virgin olive oil
2½ cups (625ml/21 fl oz) good-quality apple or pear juice
¼ cup (60ml/2 fl oz) apple cider vinegar
1 tablespoon caster (superfine) sugar
1 tablespoon juniper berries
6 sprigs sage
3 small pears, halved

Preheat oven to 200°C (400°F).

Rub salt into the pork skin and drizzle with oil.

Place the pork, skin-side down, in a deep-sided roasting pan and roast for 40 minutes.

Remove any excess fat from the pan with a spoon and discard.

Carefully turn the pork over and add the apple or pear juice, vinegar, sugar, juniper and sage to the pan and cook for a further 50 minutes or until the skin is golden and crunchy.

Add the pear to the pan and cook for a further 30 minutes or until the pears and pork are tender.

Serve the pork with the roasted pears and the pan sauce. This pork is great served with parsnip mash or a crisp fennel salad. **SERVES 4**

Cook's note: To ensure the perfect crackle, dry the pork in the refrigerator, uncovered, for 3–4 hours or until the skin feels dry to touch. Score the pork skin at 5cm intervals before rubbing with salt.

This *gently spiced rib dish* is a front-runner when it comes to flavour-packed dinners that require less effort but really *deliver the goods*. It's incredibly versatile, too – I love it with tortillas and steamed rice but it would also be great with *polenta or mash*.

smoky beef short ribs

2kg (4 lb 6 oz) beef short ribs (about 8 ribs)
sea salt and cracked black pepper
1 tablespoon extra virgin olive oil
1 brown onion, chopped
6 cloves garlic
⅓ cup (80g/2¾ oz) chipotle chillies in adobo sauce, chillies finely chopped and sauce reserved
3 cups (750ml/25½ fl oz) tomato passata (purée)
2 cups (500ml/17 fl oz) good-quality beef stock
¼ cup (60g/2 oz) firmly packed brown sugar
1 tablespoon smoked paprika
char-grilled flour tortillas, steamed rice, cooked black beans, store-bought pickled red
  onion, sliced long green chillies, coriander (cilantro) leaves and lime wedges, to serve

Heat a large ovenproof saucepan over high heat. Sprinkle the beef with salt and pepper and cook, in batches, for 2 minutes each side or until well browned. Remove from the pan and set aside.

Reduce the heat to medium–high. Add the oil and onion and cook for 4 minutes or until softened.

Add the garlic, chipotle chillies and the adobo sauce, passata, stock, sugar and paprika and stir to combine. Return the beef to the pan and bring to a rapid simmer.

Reduce the heat to low and cover with a tight-fitting lid. Cook for 3 hours–3 hours 30 minutes, turning the ribs halfway, or until tender.

Remove the lid and simmer for 20 minutes or until the sauce has thickened.

Serve with tortillas, rice, black beans, pickled onion, chilli, coriander and lime wedges. **SERVES 4**

Cook's note: I like to mash or chop the chipotle chillies and incorporate them into the adobo sauce before adding to the pan.

more than *a salad*

Sign up for *feel-good* satisfying salads that double as dinner and deliver layers of *fresh, nourishing* veggies and herbs, bold flavours and irresistible *spice and crunch.* They're the easiest of meals to throw together, and there are *countless possible variations* you can try to make each dish your own.

Zesty dressings, leafy greens and extra oomph in the form of crisp veg, crunchy nuts and a hit of spice here and there — these satisfying bowlfuls are weeknight treasures you can rely on to satisfy.

in this chapter

Chicken salads are a *simply reliable* favourite and this version mixes vibrant Thai flavours with twirls of *silky noodles* and *sticky caramelised* chicken to create the most tempting bowl.

thai caramelised chicken salad

375g (13¼ oz) dried rice noodles
1 cup (16g/½ oz) mint leaves
1 cup (16g/½ oz) coriander (cilantro) leaves
1 cup (20g/¾ oz) Thai basil leaves
2 tablespoons lime juice
½ cup (70g/2½ oz) chopped roasted unsalted cashews
1–2 long red chillies, thinly sliced
4 Thai lime leaves, thinly sliced, extra
lime wedges, to serve
caramelised chicken
½ cup (120g/4½ oz) firmly packed brown sugar
¼ cup (60ml/2 fl oz) soy sauce
¼ cup (60ml/2 fl oz) lime juice
2 tablespoons fish sauce
1½ tablespoons finely grated ginger
6 Thai lime leaves, torn
6 x 125g (4½ oz) chicken thigh fillets, trimmed and cut into chunks

To make the caramelised chicken, heat a large non-stick frying pan over medium heat.

Add the sugar, soy sauce, lime juice, fish sauce, ginger and lime leaves and stir until the sugar is dissolved. Add the chicken and cook, stirring occasionally, for 10–12 minutes or until the chicken is cooked and the sauce has reduced.

Cook the noodles according to the packet instructions. Refresh under cold water, drain and set aside. Combine the noodles, mint, coriander, basil and lime juice.

Divide the herb and noodle salad between bowls. Top with caramelised chicken, cashews, chilli and extra lime leaves and serve with lime wedges. **SERVES 4**

Cook's note: I love Thai lime leaves, but I have to go to a specialty grocer to buy them. I always buy extra and freeze whatever I don't use in a small airtight container. They discolour slightly but the unique aromatic flavour is still there when I need them for another recipe.

Every spoonful of this salad is *deliciously good*. Tender risoni, *peppery rocket,* sweet pops from currants and toasty almonds... just top with molten chilli-honey haloumi and it's *simply perfect!*

risoni and chilli-honey haloumi salad

350g (12½ oz) dried risoni
⅓ cup (80ml/2½ fl oz) lemon juice
2 tablespoons extra virgin olive oil
1 teaspoon dijon mustard
sea salt and cracked black pepper
100g (3½ oz) rocket (arugula) leaves
1 cup (16g/½ oz) mint leaves, torn
½ cup (80g/2¾ oz) toasted almonds, chopped
½ cup (50g/1¾ oz) currants
chilli-honey haloumi
1 tablespoon extra virgin olive oil
440g (15½ oz) haloumi, cut into chunks
⅓ cup (120g/4½ oz) honey
1 teaspoon dried chilli flakes

Cook the risoni in a large saucepan of salted boiling water for 8 minutes or until al dente. Drain the risoni and refresh under cold water. Set aside.

To make the chilli-honey haloumi, heat a large non-stick frying pan over medium–high heat. Add the oil and haloumi and cook for 3 minutes or until golden. Remove from the heat. Add the honey and chilli and stir to combine. Set aside.

Combine the lemon juice, oil, mustard, salt and pepper.

Place the risoni in a serving bowl. Add the rocket, mint, almond, currants and lemon mixture and toss to combine.

Top with the chilli-honey haloumi and serve. **SERVES 4**

Cook's note: The chilli-honey haloumi is best served warm. If you want to get ahead, prepare the salad components and refrigerate. Then, cook the haloumi just before serving for maximum deliciousness!

This *bold and zingy* salad gives lots of *bang for your buck*: the bang from the sichuan peppercorns, the bang from the fresh herbs and tender chicken, the *crunch from the peanuts* and veg... win!

bang bang chicken salad

2 tablespoons vegetable oil
1 tablespoon lightly crushed sichuan peppercorns
3 x 180g (6½ oz) chicken breast fillets, trimmed
sea salt flakes
5 cups (400g/14 oz) shredded wombok (chinese cabbage)
2 carrots, peeled and shredded using a julienne peeler
2 lebanese cucumbers, peeled lengthways into strips
1 cup (16g/½ oz) mint leaves
1 cup (16g/½ oz) coriander (cilantro) leaves
1–2 long red chillies, seeds removed and finely sliced lengthways
½ cup (55g/2 oz) roasted salted peanuts
extra wombok leaves (optional) and lime wedges, to serve
zingy soy dressing
⅓ cup (80ml/2½ fl oz) lime juice
¼ cup (60ml/2 fl oz) light soy sauce
1½ tablespoons caster (superfine) sugar

Heat a large non-stick frying pan over medium–high heat. Add the oil and peppercorns and cook for 10 seconds or until fragrant.

Add the chicken and cook for 1 minute, then turn over. Cover with a tight-fitting lid and reduce the heat to low. Cook for 6 minutes or until the chicken is just cooked through. Allow to stand for 5 minutes, then shred the chicken and return to the pan. Sprinkle with salt and toss to combine with the peppercorns.

To make the zingy soy dressing, combine the lime juice, soy sauce and sugar.

To assemble the salad, combine the wombok, carrot, cucumber, mint, coriander, chilli and peanuts. Spoon over the dressing and toss to coat. Arrange the salad in extra wombok leaves, if desired, on serving plates. Top with the chicken and serve with lime wedges. **SERVES 4**

Cook's note: It's worth seeking out sichuan peppercorns for this salad. They add a numbing spiciness that makes the dish unique.

This classic salad just got *supercharged!* With the addition of smoky bacon croutons and the goodness of *kale and sprouts,* it's a *delicious makeover* that gives the original a run for its money.

super green caesar with bacon croutons

2 cups (70g/2½ oz) firmly packed finely shredded kale leaves (about 2 stalks kale)

600g (1 lb 5 oz) brussels sprouts, trimmed and finely shredded

2 baby cos (romaine) lettuce, leaves separated

3 x 180g (6½ oz) cooked chicken breasts, shredded

1 cup (24g/1 oz) flat-leaf (Italian) parsley, roughly chopped

¾ cup (55g/2 oz) shaved parmesan

bacon croutons

300g (10½ oz) sourdough bread, roughly torn

2 tablespoons extra virgin olive oil

200g (7 oz) smoked bacon (about 4 rashers), trimmed and roughly chopped

caesar dressing

1 cup (250ml/8½ fl oz) buttermilk

⅓ cup (25g/1 oz) finely grated parmesan

2 tablespoons whole-egg mayonnaise

1 tablespoon dijon mustard

1 tablespoon finely chopped capers

sea salt and cracked black pepper

Preheat oven to 180°C (350°F).

To make the bacon croutons, place the torn sourdough on a tray lined with non-stick baking paper. Drizzle with oil and toss to combine. Add the bacon and cook for 20 minutes, turning occasionally, or until golden.

To make the caesar dressing, whisk to combine the buttermilk, parmesan, mayonnaise, mustard, capers, salt and pepper. Set aside.

Combine the kale, sprouts, lettuce, chicken, parsley, parmesan and dressing in a bowl and toss to coat.

To serve, place on a large platter or in a serving bowl and top with the bacon croutons. **SERVES 4**

This salad is inspired by a long-ago memory of a dish from one of my *favourite Thai restaurants* that is now sadly closed. The layers of flavours and texture are so perfect, it's easy to see why it stuck in my mind and why this version is also *unforgettable.*

poached coconut salmon salad

250g (9 oz) dried rice vermicelli noodles
4 lebanese cucumbers
1½ cups (25g/1 oz) mint leaves
1½ cups (30g/1 oz) Thai basil leaves
1–2 long green chillies, thinly sliced, extra
4 Thai lime leaves, thinly sliced, extra
⅓ cup (45g/1½ oz) roasted unsalted peanuts, roughly chopped
lime wedges, to serve
poached coconut salmon
150ml (5 fl oz) coconut milk
2 tablespoons lime juice
1½ tablespoons fish sauce
2 teaspoons finely grated ginger
2 teaspoons caster (superfine) sugar
1 long green chilli, halved
4 Thai lime leaves, lightly crushed
2 x 250g (9 oz) fillets sustainably caught salmon or ocean trout, skin removed

Cook the noodles according to the packet instructions. Refresh under cold water, drain and set aside.

To make the poached coconut salmon, heat a medium saucepan over medium heat. Add the coconut milk, lime juice, fish sauce, ginger, sugar, chilli and lime leaves and stir to combine. Bring to a simmer and cook for 4 minutes.

Add the salmon, reduce the heat to low and cook for 4 minutes each side or until cooked to your liking. Remove the salmon from the liquid and set aside to cool slightly. Strain the poaching liquid into a jug and set aside.

To assemble the salad, slice the cucumber into thirds and place on a board. Using a rolling pin, smash the cucumber into chunks and place on a serving platter.

Add the mint, basil, extra chilli, extra lime leaves and peanut and gently toss to combine. Top with the noodles and the poached salmon. Drizzle with reserved poaching liquid and serve with lime wedges. **SERVES 4**

Punchy and vibrant, chimichurri is the perfect partner for grilled meats, and doubles here as a *flavourful dressing.* Dotted over tender, juicy steak, fresh leaves and crisp tortilla strips, it gives this salad *seriously satisfying* main-meal energy.

steak salad with chimichurri dressing

4 corn tortillas, cut into thin strips
extra virgin olive oil, for drizzling
1 teaspoon sea salt flakes, plus extra for sprinkling
1 teaspoon chilli powder
½ teaspoon cracked black pepper
2 x 250g (9 oz) rump or scotch fillet steak
250g (9 oz) butter lettuce leaves
4 heirloom tomatoes, sliced
thinly sliced red onion and red-vein sorrel leaves (optional), to serve
chimichurri dressing
1 cup (24g/1 oz) flat-leaf (Italian) parsley leaves
1 cup (20g/¾ oz) coriander (cilantro) leaves
1 long green chilli, seeds removed and chopped
1 clove garlic, chopped
⅓ cup (80ml/2½ fl oz) extra virgin olive oil
2 tablespoons red wine vinegar
1 teaspoon honey
sea salt and cracked black pepper

Preheat oven to 180°C (350°F). Place the tortilla on a large baking tray lined with non-stick baking paper. Drizzle with oil, sprinkle with salt and toss to coat. Bake for 12 minutes, turning halfway, or until golden and crispy. Set aside.

Combine the salt, chilli powder and pepper. Rub the chilli mixture over the steaks and allow to marinate for 10 minutes.

Meanwhile, make the chimichurri dressing. Place the parsley, coriander, chilli, garlic, oil, vinegar, honey, salt and pepper in a small blender and blend until finely chopped. Set aside.

Heat a large non-stick frying pan on high heat. Drizzle the steak with oil and cook for 2 minutes each side or until cooked to your liking.

To assemble, slice the steaks. Place the lettuce, tomato and onion on a serving plate and top with steak and crispy tortilla. Drizzle with chimichurri dressing and top with red-vein sorrel, if desired, to serve. **SERVES 4**

Cook's note: This dressing is also great with chicken and fish.

My twist on the *classic favourite*, vitello tonnato, takes the creamy and tangy tuna dressing and layers it with potatoes and *thinly shaved fennel* to create the most *perfect, elegant salad.*

potato and fennel salad
with tonnato dressing

1kg (2 lb 3 oz) cooked baby potatoes, thickly sliced or cut in quarters
2 tablespoons extra virgin olive oil
1½ tablespoons lemon juice, extra
1 fennel, thinly sliced using a mandoline
300g (10½ oz) green beans, trimmed, halved and blanched
½ cup (80g/2¾ oz) cornichons or dill pickles, thinly sliced
¾ cup (180g/6½ oz) kalamata olives
1 cup (24g/1 oz) flat-leaf (Italian) parsley leaves
lemon wedges, to serve
tonnato dressing
⅔ cup (200g/7 oz) whole-egg mayonnaise
200g (7 oz) can tuna in oil, drained
4 anchovies
2 tablespoons capers, rinsed
¼ cup (60ml/2 fl oz) lemon juice
sea salt and cracked black pepper

To make the tonnato dressing, place the mayonnaise, tuna, anchovies, capers, lemon juice, salt and pepper in a food processor and process until almost smooth.

Place the tonnato dressing in a large bowl, add the potato and toss to coat. Place on a serving platter.

Combine the oil, extra lemon juice, salt and pepper in a large bowl. Add the fennel, beans, cornichon or pickle, olives and parsley and toss to coat.

Place the fennel salad on top of the potatoes. Sprinkle with pepper and serve with lemon wedges.
SERVES 4

Cook's note: Keep a close eye on your potatoes while they cook, as they'll get mushy if they cook for too long. I always like to take them out of the water just before they're done, when they still have a bit of bite, as they'll keep cooking a little as they cool.

This is my favourite way to eat broccoli – charred and *slightly smoky*. Combine with *nutty quinoa, salty feta,* crisp, cool cucumbers, peppery rocket, sweet currants and a creamy *green goddess dressing,* and it's a salad sensation.

charred broccoli salad with pepita green goddess dressing

750g (1 lb 11 oz) broccoli, cut into large wedges
extra virgin olive oil, for brushing
sea salt and cracked black pepper
4 cups (660g/1 lb 7 oz) cooked quinoa
½ cup (55g/2 oz) currants
180g (6½ oz) feta, thinly sliced
12 baby cucumbers, sliced
120g (4¼ oz) rocket (arugula) leaves
1 tablespoon sumac
pepita green goddess dressing
1 cup (24g/1 oz) flat-leaf (Italian) parsley leaves
½ cup (80g/2¾ oz) toasted pepitas (pumpkin seeds), plus extra to serve
2 green onions (scallions), trimmed and chopped
1 cup (250ml/8½ fl oz) water
⅓ cup (80ml/2¾ fl oz) lemon juice
2 tablespoons hulled tahini

Preheat oven grill (broiler) to high.

Brush broccoli with oil and place on a baking tray lined with non-stick baking paper.

Sprinkle with salt and pepper and grill for 10 minutes or until the edges are charred.

While the broccoli is cooking, make the pepita green goddess dressing. Place the parsley, pepitas, green onion, water, lemon juice, tahini and a little salt in a blender and blend until smooth.

To serve, combine the quinoa and currants and place on a serving platter. Top with feta, cucumber, rocket and broccoli. Sprinkle with sumac and serve with extra pepitas and green goddess dressing. **SERVES 4**

Cook's note: The dressing is delicious on all sorts of salads. Make up a double batch and store in the refrigerator for up to 5 days.

impress me
desserts

These are my glamorous sweet creations that *give all the wow* without the work. In this chapter, I promise *a little touch of indulgence* that you can create with a few easy whips, *swirls and dollops*. These simply gorgeous desserts are as impressive and irresistible as they are achievable, so be prepared to *transform your dessert playlist.*

Decadent, impressive desserts don't have to be tricky! Heavenly flavour combos, fresh fruits, indulgent ingredients that add extra creaminess, and clever techniques are here to help you shine!

in this chapter

I do *adore a tiramisu,* and this coffee-free homage to the Italian classic is *super simple,* lightened with the tangy lemon, velvety mascarpone and a little kick of limoncello. *That's la dolce vita!*

limoncello tiramisu

16 thin savoiardi (sponge finger) biscuits
mascarpone lemon curd cream
200g (7 oz) mascarpone
1 cup (250ml/8½ fl oz) pure (pouring) cream
1½ tablespoons pure icing (confectioner's) sugar, plus extra for dusting
1 teaspoon vanilla extract
½ cup (175g/6 oz) store-bought lemon curd
limoncello syrup
⅓ cup (80ml/2½ fl oz) water
2 tablespoons lemon juice
1½ tablespoons caster (superfine) sugar
⅓ cup (80ml/2½ fl oz) limoncello

To make the limoncello syrup, place the water, lemon juice and caster sugar in a small saucepan over medium heat and stir until the sugar dissolves. Simmer for 4 minutes or until the syrup slightly reduces. Refrigerate until cold. Add the limoncello and stir to combine.

To make the mascarpone lemon curd cream, place the mascarpone, cream, icing sugar and vanilla in a bowl and whisk until soft peaks form. Add the lemon curd and swirl through the cream.

To assemble, dip half the biscuits into the limoncello syrup for about 3 seconds and divide between serving plates. Top with half the mascarpone lemon curd cream, then repeat the layer with remaining biscuits and cream. Dust with icing sugar to serve. **SERVES 4**

Cook's note: To make this without the limoncello, simply replace with lemon juice and add an extra 2 tablespoons of sugar to the syrup.

This decadent cake is the true *taste of heaven* in the form of the ultra-luxe combination of honey, almonds and rosewater. The trio truly shines in this *gorgeously layered dessert* that's destined to be a showstopper at your next celebration.

honey and almond layer cake with rosewater cream

1¼ cup (450g/1 lb) honey, plus extra for drizzling
6 eggs
⅔ cup (160ml/5½ fl oz) light-flavoured extra virgin olive oil
½ cup (125ml/4 fl oz) milk
4½ cups (540g/1 lb 3 oz) almond meal (ground almonds)
1½ teaspoons baking powder, sifted
rosewater cream
2 cups (500ml/17 fl oz) pure (pouring) cream
2 cups (480g/1 lb 1 oz) crème fraîche
½ cup (80g/2¾ oz) pure icing (confectioner's) sugar
3 teaspoons rosewater

Preheat oven to 160°C (325°F). Line 2 x 20cm (8 in) round cake tins with non-stick baking paper.

Combine the honey, eggs, oil and milk and whisk to combine. Add the almond meal and baking powder and whisk until smooth.

Divide the mixture between the prepared tins and bake for 40–45 minutes or until cooked when tested with a skewer.

Allow to cool in the tin for 10 minutes, then invert onto a wire rack to cool completely.

To make the rosewater cream, whisk the cream, crème fraîche, sugar and rosewater until soft peaks form.

To serve, place one cake on a cake stand or serving plate. Top with half the rosewater cream and the remaining cake. Top with the remaining rosewater cream, smoothing the sides of the cake with a little of the cream to coat. Drizzle the cake with a little extra honey before serving.
SERVES 10–12

Cook's note: Don't be tempted to overwhip the cream — it needs to be at just-soft peaks. If it's a warm day, it helps to chill your cakes for an hour or two before topping with the rosewater cream.

This has to be the most *impressive cheat's dessert* I have up my sleeve. It's a delightful mash-up of two iconic desserts and is so much simpler than it looks – it's just store-bought ice-cream, all wrapped up in toasted meringue. *So glam, so easy.*

tiramisu baked alaska

1 x 500ml (17 fl oz) tub good-quality store-bought vanilla bean ice-cream
cocoa powder, for dusting
12–14 thin savoiardi (sponge finger) biscuits
espresso soaking liquid
¼ cup (60ml/2 fl oz) espresso, cooled
2 tablespoons coffee liqueur
Italian meringue
140ml (4½ fl oz) egg whites (about 4 eggs)
⅔ cup (150g/5½ oz) caster (superfine) sugar

To make the espresso soaking liquid, combine the espresso and coffee liqueur in a shallow bowl.

Remove the packaging from the ice-cream and place upside-down on a tray lined with non-stick baking paper. Dust the ice-cream with cocoa powder.

Dip the biscuits into the espresso soaking liquid for about 2 seconds and press around the sides of the ice-cream. Trim some biscuits to fit over the top of the ice-cream. Dust the biscuits with more cocoa powder and freeze for 30 minutes or until firm.

Meanwhile, make the Italian meringue. Place the egg whites and sugar in a heatproof bowl over a saucepan of simmering water (the bowl shouldn't touch the water). Stir with a spatula for 5 minutes or until sugar has dissolved.

Remove from the heat and transfer the mixture to the bowl of an electric mixer. Beat for 8–10 minutes or until thick and glossy.

Using a palette knife, spread the meringue over the sponge finger biscuits until completely covered. Using a kitchen blowtorch, toast the meringue until golden brown. Slice and serve.
SERVES 4

Cook's note: You can make this dessert a day ahead of time. You can either make it completely or leave the blowtorching until your guests arrive, and up the excitement by blowtorching at the table!

This *fudgy, creamy* white chocolate blondie is going to take your affogato game to *unbelievable new heights.* The ultimate dinner-party dessert, it's indulgent and rich, and when doused in an espresso syrup, *completely addictive.*

affogato blondie

125g (4½ oz) unsalted butter, softened
125g (4½ oz) white chocolate, chopped
395g (14 oz) can sweetened condensed milk
½ cup (110g/4 oz) caster (superfine) sugar
1 tablespoon vanilla extract
2 eggs
¾ cup (110g/4 oz) plain (all-purpose) flour
¼ teaspoon baking powder
vanilla bean ice-cream, to serve
espresso syrup
⅔ cup (160ml/5½ fl oz) hot espresso
¼ cup (55g/2 oz) caster (superfine) sugar

Preheat oven to 160°C (325°F). Line a 20cm (8 in) square cake tin with non-stick baking paper.

Place the butter, white chocolate, condensed milk, sugar and vanilla in a saucepan over low heat and stir until melted. Pour into a bowl.

Add the eggs and whisk to combine.

Sift over the flour and baking powder and mix until just combined.

Pour into the prepared tin and bake for 25–30 minutes or until set.

While the blondie is baking, make the espresso syrup. Heat a medium frying pan over low heat. Add the espresso and sugar and stir until the sugar dissolves. Gently simmer for 10–12 minutes or until the syrup has thickened. Do not allow the mixture to boil or it will become bitter. Set aside to cool slightly.

To serve, slice the blondie and place on serving plates. Top with ice-cream and a drizzle of the espresso syrup. **SERVES 9**

Cook's note: This blondie is beyond fudgy deliciousness so feel free to make and serve as is, without the ice-cream and syrup.

If I had to pick the cake *I love to snack on the most,* it would have to be this one. It's my current cake crush – the softness of the ricotta, the crunch of the almonds, the spiky hit of *tangy raspberry...* seriously, so good!

lemon, raspberry and almond ricotta cake

125g (4½ oz) unsalted butter, softened
1 cup (220g/8 oz) caster (superfine) sugar
2 tablespoons finely grated lemon rind
1 teaspoon vanilla extract
4 large eggs, separated
2 cups (240g/8½ oz) almond meal (ground almonds)
1 cup (240g/8½ oz) fresh ricotta
125g (4½ oz) raspberries
½ cup (50g/1¾ oz) flaked almonds
thick or double (thick) cream (optional), to serve

Preheat oven to 160°C (325°F). Line a 20cm (8 in) round cake tin with non-stick baking paper.

Place the butter and ⅔ cup (150g/5½ oz) of the sugar in the bowl of an electric mixer and beat for 4 minutes or until light and creamy. Add the lemon rind and vanilla and beat until combined.

Add the egg yolks, one at a time, beating well between each addition.

Fold through the almond meal and ricotta.

In a clean bowl of an electric mixer, whisk the egg whites until soft peaks form. Add the remaining sugar and whisk until stiff peaks form.

Fold a spoonful of whipped egg white into the almond mixture, then gently fold in the remaining egg white until combined.

Spoon the mixture into the prepared tin and sprinkle with raspberries and almonds. Bake for 1 hour or until firm and golden around the edges but with a slight jiggle in the middle. Allow the cake to cool completely in the tin.

To serve, place on a cake stand or serving plate. Serve with cream, if desired. **SERVES 10-12**

Cook's note: Don't be scared by the uncooked appearance of the centre of this cake when it's just out of the oven. As the cake cools, it will set to the most deliciously moist texture.

This is my no-fail version of a *classic tarte tatin*. Skip the tricky sugar caramel and replace it with maple syrup for *perfect caramelised fruit,* every time.

plum and vanilla tarte tatin

375g (13 oz) store-bought ready rolled puff pastry
50g (1¾ oz) unsalted butter
¼ cup (60ml/2 fl oz) pure maple syrup
1 vanilla bean, split
6 plums, deseeded and quartered
double (thick) cream or vanilla bean ice-cream, to serve

Preheat oven to 200°C (400°F).

Using a plate as a guide, cut the pastry into 2 x 22cm (9 in) rounds. Place one round on top of the other to create an extra-thick pastry. Refrigerate until required.

Heat the butter and maple in a 20cm (8 in) non-stick ovenproof frying pan over medium heat until the butter has melted.

Add the vanilla bean and bring to a simmer. Add the plums and arrange in the base of the pan. Cook for 3–4 minutes or until just soft. Remove from the heat.

Place the pastry over the plums and press down gently to secure.

Place the pan on a large baking tray and transfer to the oven. Bake for 20–25 minutes or until the pastry is puffed and golden. Allow to stand for 5 minutes.

Carefully invert onto a serving plate. Serve with cream or ice-cream. **SERVES 4**

Cook's note: The beauty of this recipe is that you can switch the plums for any other stone fruit – try apricots, peaches or nectarines.

I created this *very Australian version* of pavlova when I was celebrating a humbling achievement in my life. It's a very special recipe that reminds me why *I'm really proud to do the work I do,* and how much I love living in the place *I call home.*

lamington pavlova

280ml (9½ fl oz) egg whites (about 8 eggs)
2¼ cups (500g/1 lb 2 oz) caster (superfine) sugar
½ cup (45g/1½ oz) desiccated coconut
2 tablespoons cocoa powder
300ml (10 fl oz) pure (pouring) cream
⅓ cup (105g/3¾ oz) homemade or store-bought raspberry jam
toasted shredded coconut, to serve
chocolate sauce
100g (3½ oz) dark (70% cocoa) chocolate, chopped
300ml (10 fl oz) pure (pouring) cream, extra

Preheat oven to 150°C (300°F). Line a baking tray with non-stick baking paper.

Place the egg whites and sugar in a heatproof bowl over a saucepan of simmering water (the bowl shouldn't touch the water). Stir with a spatula for 5 minutes or until sugar has dissolved.

Remove from the heat and transfer mixture to the bowl of an electric mixer. Beat for 8–10 minutes or until thick and glossy. Add the coconut and fold through to just combine.

Spoon the meringue mixture onto the prepared tray and shape into a tall round. Sift the cocoa over the top of the meringue.

Reduce oven to 120°C (250°F) and bake for 1 hour 15 minutes or until pavlova is dry to touch. Turn off the heat and allow to cool completely in the closed oven.

Place the cream in a large bowl and whisk until soft peaks form. Add the raspberry jam and swirl through the cream. Set aside.

To make the chocolate sauce, place the chocolate and extra cream in a small saucepan over low heat and stir until the chocolate has melted. Set aside to cool.

To assemble, place the chocolate pavlova on a cake stand or serving plate. Top the pavlova with raspberry-jam cream and sprinkle with toasted shredded coconut. Serve with chocolate sauce.
SERVES 8–10

Cook's note: When making the meringue, check if the sugar has dissolved by rubbing the egg-white mixture between your fingertips. If the mixture is gritty, you need to cook the sugar mixture a little longer.

Because sometimes in life, you just want a sweet, milky chocolate cake with a whipped *creamy chocolate frosting.* Just look at those beautifully smooth and silky swirls! *Absolutely gorgeous!*

milk chocolate fudge cake with whipped chocolate frosting

250g (9 oz) unsalted butter
250g (9 oz) milk chocolate, chopped
1 cup (240g/8½ oz) firmly packed brown sugar
½ cup (110g/4 oz) caster (superfine) sugar
4 eggs
¾ cup (180ml/6 fl oz) milk
2 teaspoons vanilla extract
1½ cups (225g/8 oz) plain (all-purpose) flour
¼ cup (25g/1 oz) cocoa powder
2 teaspoons baking powder
whipped chocolate frosting
600ml (20¼ fl oz) pure (pouring) cream
300g (10½ oz) milk chocolate, finely chopped, extra

To make the whipped chocolate frosting, place the cream in a small saucepan over medium–low heat. Bring the cream to just below boiling. Remove from the heat. Place the extra chocolate in a heatproof bowl and pour over the hot cream. Stir until melted and smooth. Using a handheld stick blender, blend the chocolate mixture for 30 seconds. Refrigerate for 2–3 hours or overnight.

To make the cake, preheat oven to 160°C (325°F). Line a 22cm (9 in) round cake tin with non-stick baking paper.

Place the butter and chocolate in a small saucepan over low heat and stir until melted and smooth.

Place the sugars in a bowl, add the chocolate mixture and whisk to combine. Add the eggs, milk and vanilla and whisk to combine.

Sift over the flour, cocoa and baking powder and whisk until just combined. Spoon the mixture into the prepared tin and bake for 1 hour or until cooked when tested with a skewer. Allow the cake to cool in the tin.

Using an electric mixer, whip the chilled frosting until just soft peaks form (see *cook's tip*). Place the cake on a cake stand or serving plate and top with swirls of the whipped frosting. **SERVES 10–12**

Cook's tip: The secret to the most velvety frosting is to use a handheld stick blender to emulsify the chocolate and cream. Take care that you don't over-whip your frosting just before you ice the cake.

This *elegant centrepiece cake* will create a 'wow' moment at your next celebration. I doubled the quantities to make an even more *stunning feature,* but this recipe is perfect for a smaller crowd.

elderflower centrepiece cake with whipped white chocolate frosting

6 eggs
1½ cups (330g/11½ oz) caster (superfine) sugar
1 tablespoon vanilla extract
200g (7 oz) unsalted butter, melted
1¼ cups (150g/5½ oz) almond meal (ground almonds)
1¾ cups (260g/9 oz) plain (all-purpose) flour
3 teaspoons baking powder
edible flowers, herbs or nasturtium leaves, to decorate
pure icing (confectioner's) sugar, for dusting
elderflower syrup
½ cup (125ml/4 fl oz) elderflower cordial
2 tablespoons water
2 tablespoons caster (superfine) sugar, extra
whipped white chocolate frosting
1¾ cups (430ml/14½ fl oz) pure (pouring) cream
250g (9 oz) white chocolate, finely chopped

To make the whipped white chocolate frosting, place the cream in a small saucepan over medium–low heat. Bring the cream to just below boiling. Place the chocolate in a heatproof bowl and pour over the hot cream. Stir until smooth. Using a handheld stick blender, blend the chocolate mixture for 30 seconds. Refrigerate for 2–3 hours or overnight (see *cook's note* p208).

To make the cake, preheat oven to 160°C (325°F). Line a 8cm x 32cm (3¼ in x 12½ in) loaf tin with non-stick baking paper.

Place the eggs, caster sugar, vanilla, butter and almond meal in a large bowl. Sift over the flour and baking powder and whisk until smooth. Pour the mixture into the prepared tin and bake for 50 minutes or until cooked when tested with a skewer. Allow to cool in the tin for 10 minutes. Invert onto a wire rack.

While the cake is cooling, make the elderflower syrup. Simmer the cordial, water and extra caster sugar in a small saucepan over medium heat, stirring occasionally, for 4 minutes or until slightly reduced. Generously brush syrup over the top and sides of the hot cake. Allow to cool completely.

Using an electric mixer, whip the chilled frosting until just soft peaks form (see *cook's note* p208). Trim the top of the cake so it is flat. Place the cake on a serving plate or board, or directly onto the table on a sheet of non-stick baking paper. Top with swirls of the whipped frosting. Decorate with edible flowers, herbs or leaves and dust with icing sugar. **MAKES ONE CAKE (SERVES 10–12)**

This recipe takes humble yoghurt and transforms it into a *gorgeously creamy and indulgent* dessert. Delicately flavoured with honey, vanilla and rosewater, and with a *luxe spoonable* consistency, it makes the perfect sweet sidekick.

rhubarb and strawberries with vanilla labne

250g (9 oz) rhubarb (about 4 stalks), trimmed and cut into chunks
250g (9 oz) strawberries, trimmed
½ cup (110g/4 oz) caster (superfine) sugar
4 strips orange peel
1 vanilla bean, split and seeds scraped
vanilla labne
1kg (2 lb 3 oz) plain thick Greek yoghurt
¼ cup (90g/3 oz) honey
1 tablespoon vanilla bean paste
2 teaspoons rosewater
¼ teaspoon table salt

To make the vanilla labne, line a sieve or colander with fine muslin or clean cloth and suspend over a bowl that's deep enough for liquid to collect at the bottom without touching the base of the sieve.

Combine the yoghurt, honey, vanilla paste, rosewater and salt. Pour into the prepared muslin, gather the edges to enclose and use kitchen string to secure.

Refrigerate for 48–72 hours or until the labne is drained and reaches your preferred firmness. Discard the drained liquid.

Place the rhubarb, strawberries, sugar, orange peel and vanilla bean and seeds in a medium frying pan over medium heat. Cook for 6 minutes or until the rhubarb and strawberries are soft.

Divide the strawberries, rhubarb and syrup between bowls and serve with vanilla labne. **SERVES 6-8**

Cook's note: Serve this sweet labne for breakfast with fruit and granola or add to an after–dinner cheeseboard with crackers, nuts and sliced fresh and dried fruits.

super-fast *snacks*

These *fast, wholesome sweet fixes* are perfect for those 'I need something delicious right now' moments. With *swirls of chocolate*, sprinkles of nuts and drizzles of honey, these *easy-to-prep* cookies, brownies, bars and treats will have you on your way to *seriously addictive*, scrumptious snacks that really *hit the spot*.

When those cravings hit, this chapter gives you the answer. Decadent, wholesome treats you can prep with minimal fuss, and keep in the fridge or freezer. Your sweet tooth will thank you!

in this chapter

When you're craving just a little warm *gooey, chocolatey* sweet treat, my mini brownie *fits the bill exactly.* This perfectly molten *choc delight* is the ideal size for sharing (or not... no judgement!)

snacking brownie

½ cup (75g/2¾ oz) plain (all-purpose) flour
2 tablespoons cocoa powder
⅔ cup (160g/5½ oz) firmly packed brown sugar
60g (2 oz) unsalted butter, melted
½ teaspoon vanilla extract
1 egg
50g (1¾ oz) dark (70% cocoa) chocolate chunks
vanilla bean ice-cream, to serve

Preheat oven to 160°C (325°F). Line a 12cm (4¾ in) ovenproof skillet or frying pan with non-stick baking paper.

Combine the flour, cocoa, sugar, butter, vanilla and egg in a bowl.

Add the chocolate chunks and stir to combine.

Spoon the mixture into the prepared pan. Bake for 20–25 minutes or until the brownie is set.

Allow the brownie to cool in the pan for 2 minutes. Serve warm with ice-cream or leave to cool completely before serving. **SERVES 1–2**

Cook's note: You can also bake this brownie in a 1-cup (250ml) capacity ramekin or pie tin.

If you *love an almond croissant* as much as my boys do, you'll understand why they begged me to make a cookie version. (And these are a situation on social media apparently!) I can confirm they are *crazy delicious* – you should bake a batch immediately.

chewy almond cookies

250g (9 oz) unsalted butter, melted
1 cup (240g/8½ oz) firmly packed brown sugar
1 cup (220g/8 oz) caster (superfine) sugar
1 cup (120g/4½ oz) almond meal (ground almonds)
1 egg
2 teaspoons vanilla extract
2 cups (300g/10½ oz) plain (all-purpose) flour
1 teaspoon baking powder
1¼ cups (135g/5 oz) flaked almonds
pure icing (confectioner's) sugar, for dusting

Combine the butter, brown sugar, caster sugar, almond meal, egg and vanilla in a bowl. Sift over the flour and baking powder and stir to combine.

Place the flaked almonds on a plate. Roll 2 tablespoonfuls of the cookie dough mixture into balls and roll each ball in the flaked almonds to coat. Place on a large baking tray lined with non-stick baking paper and freeze for 30 minutes or until firm.

Preheat oven to 180°C (350°F).

In batches, place the chilled cookie balls on a large baking tray lined with non-stick baking paper, allowing for spreading. Bake for 15 minutes or until golden. Allow to cool on the tray.

Dust with icing sugar to serve. **MAKES 22**

Cook's note: If you want to bake these cookies in smaller batches, you can store the cookie dough in your freezer for up to 3 months. Allow the cookie dough balls to stand on the baking trays for 10 minutes before baking.

It's going to be a *hot popsicle summer,* so get ready with these frosty treats. They're everything you love about a creamy raspberry cheesecake, only frozen into *cooling ice pops.* I always keep a stash in the freezer for treats or entertaining.

raspberry cheesecake popsicles

250g (9 oz) cream cheese, softened and chopped
½ cup (110g/4 oz) caster (superfine) sugar
2 teaspoons vanilla extract
½ cup (125g/4½ oz) plain thick Greek yoghurt
1 cup (125g/4½ oz) frozen raspberries
plain sweet biscuits, crushed, for sprinkling

Place the cream cheese, sugar and vanilla in a blender and blend until smooth. Transfer to a bowl. Add the yoghurt and raspberries and fold to combine.

Divide the mixture between 8 x ⅓ cup (80ml/2½ fl oz)-capacity popsicle moulds. Freeze for 2 hours or until firm.

To serve, unmould the popsicles and press both sides into the biscuit crumb. Serve immediately.
MAKES 8

Cook's note: You can change up the flavours here based on whatever you love, or have to hand. Use frozen blueberries, chopped strawberries, or chopped or frozen mango.

These sweet snacks are a *more wholesome version* of a classic chocolate bar we all know and love, but I promise you, they're better! They're loaded with *creamy, nutty goodness* and soft caramelicious dates. You may become seriously addicted (sorry!).

caramel choc peanut bars

1 cup (250g/9 oz) cashew butter
1 teaspoon vanilla extract
2 tablespoons pure maple syrup
2 tablespoons coconut flour
peanut caramel layer
14 soft fresh dates (about 280g/10 oz), pitted and roughly chopped
1 tablespoon pure maple syrup, extra
2 teaspoons vanilla extract, extra
¼ cup (70g/2½ oz) smooth natural peanut butter
¼ cup (25g/1 oz) roasted salted peanuts, roughly chopped, plus extra to top
chocolate topping
150g (5½ oz) dark (70% cocoa) chocolate, melted
2 teaspoons grapeseed or vegetable oil

Line a 10cm x 21cm (4½ in x 8½ in) loaf tin with non-stick baking paper.

To make the base, combine the cashew butter, vanilla, maple and coconut flour.

Press into the prepared tin and smooth the surface, using the back of a spoon. Freeze for 15 minutes or until firm.

To make the peanut caramel layer, place the dates, extra maple and extra vanilla in a food processor and process until smooth. Transfer the date mixture to a bowl. Add the peanut butter and peanut and mix to combine. Spoon the peanut mixture over the base and smooth the surface, using the back of a spoon. Freeze for 1 hour or until firm.

To make the chocolate topping, combine the chocolate and oil. Spoon over the peanut caramel layer and tip the tin to evenly coat the top. Sprinkle with extra peanut and freeze for 20 minutes or until set. Cut into bars and store in an airtight container in the freezer for up to 3 months.
MAKES 16 BARS

Cook's note: You can swap cashew butter for almond butter or thick peanut butter. These bars only need a minute or two out of the freezer until they are soft enough to eat – if you can wait that long!

If you haven't tried the *tahini, banana and honey combo,* I'm here to tell you: your life may just be about to change. Talk about a *perfect marriage of flavours!* These fluffy pancakes are one of my go-to snacks and I just know *you'll love them, too.*

tahini banana pancakes

1¾ cup (260g/9 oz) plain (all-purpose) wholemeal (whole-wheat) flour
1 tablespoon baking powder, sifted
1½ cups (390g/14 oz) smooth mashed banana (about 4 bananas)
½ cup (125ml/4 fl oz) milk
1 egg
⅓ cup (90g/3 oz) hulled tahini
¼ cup (90g/3 oz) honey, plus extra to serve

Combine the flour and baking powder. Combine the banana, milk, egg, tahini and honey in a separate bowl.

Add the banana mixture to the flour mixture and mix to combine.

Heat a non-stick frying pan over medium–low heat.

In batches, add ⅓-cupfuls (80ml/2½ fl oz) of mixture and cook for 2–3 minutes each side or until cooked. Drizzle with extra honey to serve. **MAKES 12**

Cook's note: To ensure maximum fluffiness, this mixture is best cooked straight after preparing. My cooking guide is low and slow, so don't be tempted to turn up the heat!

These snaps are reminiscent of those *sweet Florentine biscuits* that were a hit when I was younger. This time around, I've made them with all the *healthy nuts and seeds* your body needs, and drizzled them with the dark chocolate you crave. Yum!

choc almond cashew snaps

¾ cup (120g/4½ oz) chopped raw almond
¾ cup (105g/3½ oz) chopped raw cashew
½ cup (80g/2¾ oz) pepitas (pumpkin seeds)
½ cup (80g/2¾ oz) sunflower seeds
⅓ cup (80ml/2½ fl oz) pure maple syrup
2 tablespoons hulled tahini
2 teaspoons vanilla extract
60g (2oz) dark (70% cocoa) chocolate, melted
sea salt flakes, to serve (optional)

Preheat oven to 160°C (325°F). Line 2 baking trays with non-stick baking paper.

Combine the almond, cashew, pepitas, sunflower seeds, maple, tahini and vanilla.

Place 2 heaped tablespoons of the mixture onto prepared trays and flatten. Bake for 15 minutes or until golden. Allow to cool on the trays.

Drizzle each cluster with chocolate and sprinkle with sea salt, if desired. Refrigerate for 30 minutes or until set. **MAKES 16**

Cook's note: Swap the nuts and seeds as you wish. Be adventurous and try sesame seeds, walnuts, pecans or peanuts. These will keep in an airtight container for up to 5 days.

If you love a certain *famous chocolate hazelnut ball,* welcome to the *better-for-you version* that will blow your taste buds away. And, it's a cinch to make, I promise. *You're welcome!*

choc hazelnut slice

1 cup (140g/5 oz) blanched hazelnuts, roasted
1 cup (120g/4½ oz) almond meal (ground almonds)
12 soft fresh dates (about 240g/8½ oz), pitted and chopped
¼ cup (60g/2 oz) almond butter
¼ cup (25g/1 oz) cocoa powder
2 tablespoons pure maple syrup
2 teaspoons vanilla extract
choc almond topping
150g (5½ oz) dark (70% cocoa) chocolate, chopped
2 tablespoons almond butter, extra

Line a 10cm x 21cm (4½ in x 8½ in) loaf tin with non-stick baking paper.

Place the hazelnuts and almond meal in a food processor and process for 30 seconds or until finely chopped.

Add the dates, almond butter, cocoa, maple and vanilla and process for 30 seconds or until very finely chopped and the mixture is starting to form a rough dough.

Press into the prepared tin and smooth the surface, using the back of a spoon. Refrigerate for 30 minutes or until cold.

To make the choc almond topping, place the chocolate and extra almond butter in a heatproof bowl over a saucepan of simmering water (the bowl shouldn't touch the water) and stir until melted.

Pour the choc almond topping over the choc hazelnut layer and refrigerate for 30 minutes or until set. Cut into slices to serve. Store in an airtight container in the refrigerator for up to 10 days. **MAKES 12**

Cook's note: After coating the slice with chocolate, tap it gently on the benchtop to remove any air bubbles and to give the slice a smooth finish. You can use cashew or peanut butter in place of the almond butter if you prefer.

If you're looking for the perfect 3pm hit of *super-satisfying sweet caramel,* I have you covered. These moreish bliss balls with a *smooth date-caramel centre* and a creamy coconut-cashew coating are the perfect sweet treat.

coconut and date caramel bliss balls

¾ cup (60g/2 oz) desiccated coconut, plus extra for rolling
1 cup (250g/9 oz) cashew butter
⅓ cup (50g/1¾ oz) coconut sugar
1 tablespoon coconut flour
1 tablespoon vanilla extract, extra
date caramel
6 soft fresh dates (about 120g/4½ oz), pitted and very finely chopped
¼ cup (60g/2 oz) cashew butter
1 tablespoon pure maple syrup
1 teaspoon vanilla extract

To make the date caramel, place the dates in a food processor and process for 30 seconds or until almost smooth. Add the cashew butter, maple and vanilla and process until smooth. Place 16 teaspoonfuls of the mixture on a tray lined with non-stick baking paper and freeze for 30 minutes or until firm.

Combine the desiccated coconut, cashew butter, coconut sugar, coconut flour and extra vanilla and mix well.

Place the extra desiccated coconut in a bowl.

Roll tablespoonfuls of the coconut and cashew butter mixture into 16 patties. Place 1 piece of the prepared date caramel in the centre of each patty and gently roll into a ball to enclose.

Roll each ball in the coconut to cover and place on a tray. Refrigerate for 30 minutes or until firm.

Store in an airtight container in the refrigerator for up to 10 days. **MAKES 16**

Cook's note: If you want to make a big batch, they are best stored in the freezer in an airtight container. They only need a few minutes to defrost to the perfect creamy consistency before eating.

When you can't find the *healthy snack bar* you want in the supermarket, make these! They tick all the boxes: nut-free for *kids' lunchboxes,* sweetened with banana and maple, and full of energy, fibre, prebiotics and antioxidants. Not to forget, *they're absolutely delicious!*

oaty banana coconut energy bars

1 cup (260g/9 oz) smooth mashed banana (about 3 bananas)
½ cup (125ml/4 fl oz) light-flavoured extra virgin olive oil or flaxseed oil
⅔ cup (160ml/5½ fl oz) pure maple syrup
2 cups (180g/6½ oz) rolled oats
1 cup (100g/3½ oz) desiccated coconut
½ cup (100g/3½ oz) dried blueberries
2 tablespoons psyllium husks
2 teaspoons ground cinnamon
2 teaspoons vanilla extract
¼ teaspoon baking powder, sifted

Preheat oven to 180°C (350°F). Line a 20cm (8 in) square cake tin with non-stick baking paper.

Place the banana, oil and maple in a large bowl and mix to combine.

Add the oats, coconut, blueberries, psyllium, cinnamon, vanilla and baking powder and mix to combine.

Pour mixture into the prepared tin and bake for 35–40 minutes or until golden brown.

Cool in the tin for 10 minutes, then transfer to a wire rack. Slice into bars and serve warm, or cool completely. Store in an airtight container in the refrigerator for up to 10 days.

MAKES 10 BARS

Cook's note: These bars are moist and delicious, so if you aren't eating them within a few days, you'll need to refrigerate or freeze to keep them fresh.

Say hello to *blueberry muffin meets sweet apple crumble.*
I've made a lot of muffins in my time and, I promise you, these
are *insanely good* and worth adding to your rotation – they also
freeze well, so satisfying snacks are always *just moments away.*

apple and blueberry crumble muffins

2½ cups (375g/13 oz) plain (all-purpose) wholemeal (whole-wheat) flour, extra

1 cup (240g/8½ oz) firmly packed brown sugar

3 teaspoons baking powder, sifted

1 teaspoon ground cinnamon

1¼ cups (310g/11 oz) plain thick Greek yoghurt

⅔ cup (160ml/5½ fl oz) light-flavoured extra virgin olive oil or vegetable oil

2 eggs

3 apples, peeled and chopped

1 cup (125g/4½ oz) fresh or frozen blueberries

crumble topping

⅓ cup (50g/1¾ oz) plain (all-purpose) wholemeal (whole-wheat) flour

¼ cup (25g/1 oz) rolled oats

2 tablespoons raw caster (superfine) sugar

40g (1½ oz) cold unsalted butter

Preheat oven to 180°C (350°F). Line a 12-hole muffin tin with paper cases.

To make the crumble topping, combine the flour, oats and sugar. Add the butter and rub between your fingertips until combined and crumbly. Set aside.

Combine the flour, sugar, baking powder and cinnamon.

In a separate jug, whisk the yoghurt, oil and eggs.

Stir the yoghurt mixture into the flour mixture. Fold through the apple and blueberries.

Divide the mixture between paper cases and top each with the crumble topping. Bake for 30–35 minutes or until cooked when tested with a skewer.

Allow to cool in the tin for 5 minutes before serving warm, or place on a wire rack to cool completely. Store in an airtight container in the refrigerator for up to 5 days. **MAKES 12**

Cook's note: If you want to change up the flavours, swap blueberries for raspberries or blackberries, and apple for pears.

things you might need to know

glossary &
index

Here you'll find basic information on some of the *useful ingredients* used throughout this book, an index of recipes, plus a handy list of *global measures, temperatures, weights* and *common conversions.*

almond

butter
This paste is made from ground almonds and is available at most supermarkets and health food stores. It's a popular alternative to peanut butter for those with peanut allergies (always check the label). Sometimes sold as 'spreads', the nut butters called for in this book are all-natural with no additives.

flaked
These skinned almonds that have been cut into delicate, paper-thin slices are used in baking and to decorate cakes.

meal (ground almonds)
Almond meal is available from most supermarkets. Take care not to confuse it with almond flour, which has a much finer texture. Make your own almond meal by processing whole almonds to a meal in a food processor – 125g (4½ oz) almonds should give 1 cup of almond meal.

slivered
Used as a topping in baking, slivered almonds are skinned almonds that have been cut lengthways into small pieces.

baking powder
A raising agent used in baking, consisting of bicarbonate of soda and/or cream of tartar. Most are gluten free (check the label). Baking powder that's kept beyond its use-by date can lose effectiveness.

bay leaves
These aromatic leaves of the bay tree are available both fresh from some greengrocers and dried from the spice section of supermarkets. Add to soups, stews and stocks for a savoury depth of flavour. Remove before serving.

beans

black beans
Popular in Latin American cuisine, these small shiny beans have a dense, meaty texture and are commonly used in Mexican dishes and salads. Available canned at most supermarkets.

butter beans (lima beans)
Large, plump white beans also known as lima beans. They go well in soups, stews and salads. Available from delicatessens and supermarkets either canned or in dried form. Dried beans need to be soaked in water before cooking, and canned simply rinsed and drained.

blanching
Blanching is a cooking method used to slightly soften the texture, heighten the colour and enhance the flavour of vegetables. Plunge the ingredient briefly into boiling unsalted water, remove and refresh under cold water. Drain well.

butter
Unless it says otherwise in a recipe, butter should be at room temperature for cooking. It should not be half-melted or too soft to handle. We mostly prefer unsalted butter, but use salted if you wish.

buttermilk
Despite its name, buttermilk contains no butter. It has a light, creamy and slightly tangy flavour. It contains cultures and acids that react with raising agents to produce carbon dioxide, which creates light and fluffy cakes, scones and pancakes. It is also great as a marinade as it tenderises meats.

cabbage

green
Pale green or white with tightly bound, waxy leaves, these common cabbages are sold whole or halved in supermarkets and are perfect for use in slaws. Choose heads that are firm and unblemished with crisp leaves that are tightly packed.

sugarloaf
A sweeter variety of cabbage, sugarloaf is bright green and has a pointier head and more tender texture than other types of cabbage.

wombok (Chinese)
Also known as napa cabbage or Chinese cabbage, wombok is elongated in shape with ribbed green-yellow leaves. It's regularly used in noodle salads and to make kimchi. Find it at most supermarkets.

capers
These small green flower buds of the caper bush are packed either in brine or salt. Capers lend their salty-sour intensity to sauces, seafood and pastas. Before using, rinse thoroughly, drain and pat dry.

cashew butter
This paste is made from ground cashews and is available at most supermarkets and health food stores. Often sold as 'spreads', the nut butters called for in this book are all-natural with no additives. Popular in baking recipes, cashew butter often gives cookies and slices a fudgy texture.

cheese

bocconcini
Bite-sized balls of the white, fresh, mild Italian cheese, mozzarella. Sold in tubs in a lightly salted brine, bocconcini spoils easily so is best consumed within 2–3 days.

burrata
An Italian stretched-curd cheese made from mozzarella, with a creamy, milky centre. It's best served simply, with something like a tomato or fig salad. It's available from most delicatessens and supermarkets.

cream cheese
A fresh, salted, spreadable cheese sold in tubs or foil-wrapped blocks. Mostly used as a spread for sandwiches and bagels, or as the base for cream cheese frosting that tops carrot cakes and muffins.

feta
A brined white cheese typically bought in blocks. Greek in origin, feta has a salty, tangy flavour ranging from mild to sharp. Traditionally made using sheep's milk, these days you can find many cow's milk versions. Use it fresh in salads, as a salty hit of creaminess over vegies, or baked.

fresh mozzarella (buffalo)
This much-loved variety of fresh Italian mozzarella is made from water buffalo's milk and/or cow's milk. Creamy and salty, it's sold in rounds, or balls, at grocers and delicatessens and is often torn into pieces and scattered over caprese salads, pizza and pasta.

gruyère
A firm cow's milk cheese with a smooth ivory interior and a natural brushed rind. Popular in Switzerland as a table cheese and cooked into fondues, gratins and quiches. It makes a fabulous melting cheese, especially in toasted sandwiches.

haloumi
A firm white Cypriot cheese made from sheep's milk, haloumi has a stringy texture and is usually sold in brine. Slice and pan-fry until golden and heated through for a salty addition to roast vegetables or salads. Buy haloumi at delicatessens and supermarkets.

manchego
Firm ivory-yellow cheese of Spanish origin made from sheep's milk. It has a subtle, buttery flavour. Buy manchego at delicatessens and supermarkets.

mascarpone
A fresh Italian triple-cream curd-style cheese, mascarpone has a smooth consistency, similar to thick (double) cream. Available in tubs from delicatessens and most supermarkets, it's used in sauces and desserts such as tiramisu, as well as in icings and frostings, for its luscious creaminess and subtle tang.

parmesan
Italy's favourite hard, granular cheese is made from cow's milk. Parmigiano Reggiano is the best variety, made under strict guidelines in the Emilia-Romagna region and aged for an average of two years. Grana Padano mainly comes from Lombardy and is aged for around 15 months.

ricotta
A creamy, finely grained white cheese. Ricotta means 'recooked' in Italian, a reference to the way the cheese is produced by heating the whey leftover from making other cheese varieties. It's fresh, creamy and low in fat and there is also a reduced-fat version, which is lighter again. Choose fresh ricotta from your delicatessen or supermarket deli.

chickpeas (garbanzo beans)
A legume native to western Asia and across the Mediterranean, chickpeas are used in soups, stews, and are the base ingredient in hummus. Dried chickpeas need soaking before use; buy them canned to skip this step.

chillies
There are more than 200 different types of chillies, or chilli peppers, in the world. Long red or green chillies are generally milder, fruitier and sweeter, while small chillies are much hotter. Remove the membranes and seeds for a milder result.

chipotle in adobo sauce
Chipotle are smoke-dried jalapeño chillies, and adobo sauce is a rich, earthy and slightly sweet sauce made from dried chillies, vinegar, garlic, oregano and other spices. It is sold in cans or jars at supermarkets, specialty grocers and delicatessens. Chipotle in adobo is popular in Mexican cuisine and also adds a great kick when stirred through mayonnaise, in tacos or tortillas, or to add punchy flavour to patties, meat dishes, or anywhere you would add chillies.

crispy chilli oil or chilli crisp
Sold in jars, crispy chilli oil or chilli crisp is a spicy infused-oil condiment. It's often a mix of chilli, oil, crunchy garlic and shallot, and other flavourings, with a mix of textures. It's a great way to add punch, spice and flavour to a huge variety of dishes, such as noodles, eggs or rice-based recipes.

dried flakes
Peppery and hot, dried chilli flakes are used as a finishing garnish, or to make chilli-based condiments and oils.

jalapeños
These dark green plump Mexican chillies are known for their medium heat and fresh, bitey flavour. Buy jalapeños sliced in jars, pickled or fresh. They're often used in Mexican cuisine, like in tacos or to give salsas a fiery edge. Much of their heat is held in the seeds and membranes, which can be removed if you prefer a milder intensity.

Chinese five-spice
An aromatic spice blend that usually features star-anise, clove, cinnamon, fennel seeds and sichuan peppercorns, Chinese five-spice is used widely across Chinese and Asian cooking to flavour meats and stir-fries.

chocolate
dark
Rich and semi-sweet, regular dark chocolate starts with around 45–55% cocoa solids. It's sold in blocks and is ideal for use in baking. I prefer using dark chocolate that has 70% cocoa solids as it has a more intense flavour.

melted
To melt chocolate, place the required amount of chopped chocolate in a heatproof bowl over a saucepan of simmering water (the bowl shouldn't touch the water). Stir until smooth.

milk
Sweet and smooth, with a paler colour than dark chocolate, milk chocolate is the most popular for eating. It usually contains around 25% cocoa solids.

white
Made from cocoa butter and milk solids, white chocolate is super sweet and creamy in colour.

chorizo
Originating in Spain, this fermented, cured and spiced pork sausage imparts a smoky, meaty flavour to dishes. Mexican chorizo is often made using fresh pork while Spanish varieties use smoked pork and feature pimenton (Spanish paprika).

coconut
coconut cream
The cream that rises to the top after the first pressing of coconut milk, coconut cream is higher both in energy and fat than regular coconut milk. It's a common ingredient in curries and Asian sweets.

desiccated
Desiccated coconut is coconut meat that has been finely shredded and dried to remove its moisture. It's unsweetened and very powdery. Great for baking as well as savoury Asian sauces and sambals.

flour
See *flour (coconut)*, p242.

coconut milk
A milky, sweet liquid made by soaking grated fresh coconut flesh or desiccated coconut and squeezing it through muslin or cheesecloth. Coconut milk shouldn't be confused with coconut water, which is the clear liquid found inside young coconuts.

shredded
In slightly larger pieces than desiccated, shredded coconut is great for adding a bit more texture to slices and cakes, or for making condiments to serve with curries.

sugar
See *sugar (coconut)*, p245.

cream
The fat content of these different varieties of creams determines their names and uses.

crème fraîche
A rich, tangy, fermented cream, traditionally from France, with a minimum fat content of 35%. Available at grocers, delicatessens and most supermarkets.

double (thick)
Often called heavy or dollop cream, double cream has a butter fat content of 40–50%. It's usually served as a side with warm puddings, pies and rich cakes.

pure (pouring) cream
With a butter fat content of 20–30%, this thin cream is the variety most commonly used in savoury cooking, and in desserts like ice-cream, panna cotta and custard. It can be whipped to a light and airy consistency. It's also called single or whipping cream.

curry paste
The store-bought curry pastes called for in this book are Thai-style and Indian. Whether red or green, choose a good-quality paste for superior results. Available from the international section of most supermarkets.

dates
With their smooth, sticky texture and deep caramel flavour, Medjool dates, referred to in this book as soft fresh dates, are called for in baked and raw treats. Not to be confused with dried dates, which have undergone a heating process.

edamame
Find these tasty, tender soy beans ready-podded in the freezer section of major greengrocers, Asian grocers and supermarkets. They are a great addition to salads, stir-fries and pastas, or used like you would other legumes in fritters.

fish sauce
This amber-coloured liquid drained from salted, fermented fish is used to add flavour to Thai, Vietnamese and Southeast Asian dishes, such as curries, noodles and salads, plus dressings and dipping sauces.

flour
buckwheat
Despite its name, buckwheat flour isn't from a grain but is milled from the seed of a plant related to rhubarb and sorrel. Often used in pancakes and noodles for its rich, nutty flavour and wholesome benefits, it's also used as a gluten-free flour substitute in cakes.

coconut
A gluten-free flour made from very finely ground dried coconut meat. It looks like plain flour but has a very different taste, as it has the nutty and sweet flavours of coconut. It can not be swapped like for like in recipes.

cornflour (cornstarch)
When made from ground corn or maize, cornflour is gluten free. Recipes often require it to be blended with water or stock for use as a thickening agent. Not to be confused with cornflour in the United States, which is actually finely ground corn meal.

plain (all-purpose)
Ground from the endosperm of wheat, plain white flour contains no raising agent and is the most commonly used flour.

rice
Rice flour is a fine flour made from ground rice. Available in white and brown varieties, it's often used as a thickening agent in baking, in cookies and shortbreads, and to coat foods when cooking Asian dishes. It's gluten free and available in supermarkets and health food stores. Not to be confused with rice starch.

wholemeal (whole-wheat)
Ground from the whole grain of wheat and thus keeping more of its nutrients and fibre, this flour is available in plain (all-purpose) and self-raising (self-rising) varieties from supermarkets and health food stores.

furikake
This nutty, crunchy, flavourful Japanese seasoning is typically made from toasted sesame seeds, nori, salt and sugar. It is widely used in Japanese cuisine to season rice and noodles, but also adds great flavour and texture to pasta, proteins and stir-fries. Find it in the Asian section of supermarkets or in Asian supermarkets. If you can't find it, use shredded nori sheets and sesame seeds instead.

gochujang
This is a spicy, savoury and slightly sweet red chilli paste originating in Korea, made from fermented rice, wheat and red chillies. Find it in the Asian section of the supermarket or in Asian supermarkets.

green onions (scallions)
Both the white and green part(s) of these long mild onions are used in salads, as a garnish and in Asian cooking. Sold in bunches, they give a fresh bite to dishes. Find them at the supermarket, Asian supermarkets or greengrocers.

harissa
A northern African red chilli paste made from chilli, garlic and spices including coriander, caraway and cumin. Available in jars and tubes from supermarkets and specialty stores. If you can't find it, use another mild-to-medium red chilli paste.

hoisin sauce
This thick, sweet and salty sauce is used extensively in Chinese cuisine. It is a dark soy-based sauce that can be used as a glaze, in sauces and as a dipping sauce. Find it in the Asian section in the supermarket.

juniper berries
The aromatic and bitter dried berries of a hardy evergreen bush, juniper is used for pickling vegetables, flavouring sauces and, most famously, for infusing gin.

kimchi
A side dish of salted and fermented vegetables that are often cabbage based, kimchi is Korean by origin, but is now popular across the western world thanks to a salty-sour flavour profile that offers a spicy tanginess to meals. Find it at some supermarkets, at Asian grocers or specialty stores.

lemongrass
A tall, lemon-scented grass used in Asian cooking. Peel away the outer leaves and chop the tender white root-end finely, or add in large pieces during cooking and remove before serving. If adding in larger pieces, bruise them with the back of a kitchen knife. Often used in curry pastes for its fragrant flavour profile. Find it at supermarkets and grocers.

maple syrup
A sweetener made from the sap of the maple tree. Be sure to use pure maple syrup. Imitation or pancake syrup is made from corn syrup flavoured with maple and does not have the same intensity of flavour. The maple syrup referred to throughout this book is pure maple syrup, free from additives and preservatives.

mirin (Japanese rice wine)
Mirin is a pale yellow, sweet and tangy Japanese cooking wine made from glutinous rice and alcohol.

miso paste
Miso is a traditional Japanese ingredient produced by fermenting rice, barley or soy beans to a paste. It's used for sauces, spreads and pickling vegetables, and is often mixed with dashi stock to serve as miso soup. Sometimes labelled simply 'miso', white, yellow and red varieties are available, their flavour increasing in intensity with their colour. The recipes in this book call for white (shiro) miso for its delicate flavour and colour. Find miso paste in supermarkets and Asian grocers.

mushrooms
oyster
This shell-shaped mushroom, sometimes called abalone, has a delicate flavour and tender bite. Colours range from pearly

white to apricot-pink. Tear, rather than cut, and cook gently, whether simmering in soups, pan-frying or grilling. Be aware that when eaten raw they can, at times, trigger an allergic reaction.

shiitake
Tan to dark brown with a meaty texture and earthy taste akin to wild mushrooms. Its dried form, found in Asian food stores, gives the most intense flavour.

noodles
Most fresh noodles will keep in the fridge for up to a week. Keep a supply of dried noodles in the pantry for last-minute meals. Available from supermarkets and Asian food stores.

dried rice
Fine, dried (stick) noodles common in Southeast Asian cooking. Depending on their thickness, rice noodles need only be boiled briefly, or soaked in hot water until soft.

fresh egg
Made from wheat flour, water and egg, these springy, chewy noodles are sold fresh in the fridge section of supermarkets or Asian grocers.

rice vermicelli
Very thin dried rice noodles sometimes called rice sticks. They are usually used in soups such as laksa, in rice paper rolls and in salads.

nori
Thin sheets of dried, vitamin-packed seaweed used in Japanese-style dishes and to wrap sushi. Available in packets from supermarkets and Asian food stores.

oil
extra virgin olive
Graded according to its flavour, aroma and acidity. Extra virgin is the highest-quality olive oil; it contains no more than 1% acid. Virgin is the next best; it contains 1.5% or less acid. Bottles labelled simply 'olive oil' contain a blend of refined and unrefined virgin olive oil. 'Light' olive oil is the least pure in quality and shouldn't be confused with light-flavoured extra virgin olive oil.

flaxseed
This oil is made from ground flaxseeds. It has a mild, nutty aroma reminiscent of sunflower or sesame seeds, and tastes crisp and mildly nutty.

grapeseed
A by-product of winemaking, grapeseed oil is made using the pressed seeds of grapes. It has a surprisingly neutral flavour. Choose grapeseed oil that has been cold-pressed. Find it at most supermarkets.

light-flavoured extra virgin olive
This is still the highest-quality olive oil and is made from a pure blend of the oil from milder-flavoured olives.

sesame
Pressed from sesame seeds, sesame oil is used in Asian cuisine more as a nutty, full-flavoured seasoning than a cooking medium.

vegetable
Oils sourced from plants or seeds, with very mild, unobtrusive flavours. Often called for in baking recipes or Asian dishes for this reason. Look out for palm oil on the label of your oil.

olive tapenade
A bold, zippy dip or spread made from finely chopped olives and other seasonings such as parsley, capers, olive oil, garlic and lemon juice. It's full of salty, briny flavour, and is a great spread for crackers. Use it to add punch to a variety of recipes.

panko (Japanese) breadcrumbs
These breadcrumbs have a drier, flakier texture than regular breadcrumbs. Widely used in Japanese cuisine and to produce crumbs for meats and vegetables.

paprika, smoked
Unlike Hungarian paprika, the Spanish style, known as pimentón, is deep and smoky. It is made from smoked, ground pimento peppers and comes in varying intensities, from sweet and mild (dulce) to bittersweet medium hot (agridulce) and hot (picante). The variety called for in this book is sweet smoky.

pastry
Make your own or use one of the many store-bought varieties, including shortcrust and filo, which are sold frozen in blocks or ready-rolled into pastry sheets. Defrost in the fridge before use.

filo
This very thin, delicate pastry is known for crisping up well when baked in the oven. It is used widely in sweet and savoury dishes such as pies and baklava. In this book, we prefer using store-bought filo from the fridge section of the supermarket rather than frozen filo, as it's easier to work with. To keep filo from drying out, cover with a clean damp tea towel while it is out of the fridge.

puff and butter puff
This pastry is quite difficult to make, so many cooks opt to use store-bought puff pastry. It can be bought in blocks from patisseries, and is sold in sheets in supermarkets. Butter puff pastry is very light and flaky, perfect for savoury and sweet pies and tarts. Often labelled 'all butter puff', good-quality sheets are usually thicker. If you can only buy thin sheets, stack two regular thawed sheets together.

shortcrust
Shortcrust pastry is a savoury or sweet pastry that is available ready-made in blocks and frozen sheets in supermarkets.

pepitas (pumpkin seeds)
Pumpkin seeds are hulled to reveal these dark green kernels that, once dried, are nutty in flavour and easy to use in smoothies, baking and salads. Find them in supermarkets.

pickled ginger
Also known as gari, this Japanese condiment is made from young ginger that's been pickled in sugar and vinegar. It's commonly served with Japanese food as a palate cleanser, but is becoming popular as a tangy addition to sushi bowls and salads. Buy it in jars from Asian grocers and supermarkets.

pita bread
A yeast-leavened round flatbread made from wheat flour, common in Mediterranean and Middle Eastern cuisine, and neighbouring regions. Often served lightly toasted to wrap up meat and vegies, it is sold at supermarkets and bakeries.

pomegranate molasses
A concentrated syrup made from pomegranate juice, with a sweet, tart flavour, pomegranate molasses is available from some supermarkets, delicatessens, Middle Eastern grocery stores and specialty food shops. If you can't find it, try using caramelised balsamic vinegar.

pomegranate seeds

The small pink seeds from inside the pomegranate, featuring a sweet and slightly tart flavour. Commonly used in desserts or salads. To extract the seeds, cut the pomegranate in half, hold it over a bowl and, using a wooden spoon, smack the skin firmly until the seeds pop out.

psyllium husks

The husks of psyllium seeds are available in health food shops and some supermarkets. Super-rich in fibre, they're used in gluten-free baking as a binding ingredient.

quinoa

Packed with protein, this grain-like seed has a chewy texture, nutty flavour and is fluffy when cooked. Use it as you would couscous or rice. It freezes well, so any excess cooked quinoa can be frozen in individual portions. Red and black varieties, which require a slightly longer cooking time, are also available in most supermarkets. 1 cup cooked white quinoa weighs 160g (5½ oz). Directions for cooking quinoa are as follows.

1 cup (180g) white quinoa
1¼ cups (310ml) water
sea salt flakes

Place the quinoa, water and a pinch of salt in a medium saucepan over high heat. Bring to the boil, cover immediately with a tight-fitting lid and reduce the heat to low. Simmer for 12 minutes or until almost tender. Remove from the heat and allow to steam for 8 minutes or until tender. **MAKES 2¾ CUPS (440G)**

ras el hanout

A North African spice mix, literally translating as 'top of the shop', ras el hanout can contain more than 20 different spices – most commonly cinnamon, cardamom, coriander, cloves, chilli, paprika and turmeric. Find it at spice shops, gourmet grocers and most supermarkets.

rice
arborio

Rice with a short, plump-looking grain that cooks to a soft texture, while retaining a firm interior. It has surface starch that creates a creamy texture in risottos when cooked al dente. It can also be used in rice pudding. Arborio is available at most supermarkets.

basmati

A type of long-grain aromatic white rice that retains its long slender length when cooked and contains higher levels of protein than regular white rice. Available at supermarkets.

brown

Brown rice is different to white rice in that the bran and germ of the wholegrain are intact. This renders it nutritionally superior and gives it a nutty chewiness. It's available at supermarkets. 1 cup cooked brown rice weighs 200g (7 oz). Directions for cooking brown rice are as follows.

1 cup (200g) brown rice
1½ cups (375ml) water
sea salt flakes

Place the rice, water and a pinch of salt in a medium saucepan over high heat. Bring to the boil, immediately cover with a tight-fitting lid and reduce the heat to low. Simmer for 25 minutes or until almost tender. Remove from the heat and allow to steam for 10 minutes or until tender. **MAKES 2 CUPS (400G)**

carnaroli

Carnaroli is used for making risotto, and although it is very similar to arborio, it has a higher starch content and firmer texture, and a slightly longer grain. Available at some supermarkets and specialty food stores.

jasmine

A long-grain white rice popular for its shape-holding, slender grains and fragrant scent. Available at supermarkets.

rosewater

An essence distilled from rose petals, rosewater is one of the cornerstone flavours of Indian and Middle-Eastern tables. Usually used in sweets, it's the distinctive flavour in Turkish delight (lokum).

sesame seeds

These small seeds have a nutty flavour and can be used in savoury and sweet cooking. White sesame seeds are the most common variety, but black, or unhulled, seeds are popular for coatings in Asian cooking.

shichimi togarashi

Also known as Japanese seven-spice or simply as togarashi, this zesty spice blend is sprinkled over rice, noodle and meat dishes. Find it in the Asian section of some supermarkets or at Asian grocers.

shiso leaves

Sometimes called perilla, this herb comes in both green-and purple-leafed varieties. It has a slight peppery flavour and is often used to wrap ingredients. The micro variety makes a pretty garnish. Find it at some greengrocers and Asian markets.

sichuan peppercorns

Sometimes called szechuan pepper or Chinese prickly ash, this Chinese pepper is commonly used in Sichuan cuisine. They offer an intense, numbing, tingling spiciness, which mellows a little when the pepper is toasted and crushed. Sichuan peppers add a deep spicy flavour to Asian dishes such as noodles and stir-fries. Find them at some supermarkets and Asian grocers.

sorrel leaves

This leafy green has a signature sour flavour. Use red-veined leaves as a pretty addition to salads or as a leafy garnish. Find red-veined sorrel leaves at your local greengrocer.

sourdough bread

A naturally leavened bread that uses a 'starter' – a fermented flour and water mixture that contains wild yeast and good bacteria – to rise, giving it a slightly chewy texture and a tangy flavour. Sourdough is also often free from additives. It's used widely in this book to make breadcrumbs for its sturdiness, and for making crunchy croutons.

sponge finger biscuits

Sweet and light Italian finger-shaped biscuits, also known as savoiardi. Great for desserts such as tiramisu because they absorb other flavours and soften well, yet at the same time maintain their shape. Available in both large and small versions at supermarkets.

sriracha hot chilli sauce

A hot sauce containing chilli, salt, sugar, vinegar and garlic, sriracha is both the brand name of a popular American blend as well as the generic name for the Southeast Asian sauce. Find it in supermarkets.

sugar

Extracted as crystals, usually from the juice of the sugar cane plant, sugar is a sweetener, flavour enhancer and food preservative.

brown

In Australia, what is known as 'brown sugar' is referred to as 'light brown sugar' in other parts of the world. Light and dark brown sugars are made from refined sugar with natural molasses added. Light and dark types are interchangeable if either is unavailable. They are an important ingredient in cookies, puddings, dense cakes and brownies. You can find both varieties of brown sugar in supermarkets.

caster (superfine)
The superfine granule of caster sugar gives baked products a light texture and crumb, which is important for many cakes and delicate desserts. Caster sugar is essential for making meringue, as the fine crystals dissolve more easily in the whipped egg white.

coconut
With an earthy, butterscotch flavour, coconut sugar, or coconut palm sugar, comes from the flowers of the coconut palm. Coconut sugar gives a lovely depth of flavour. Find it in select supermarkets, and at Asian grocers.

icing (confectioner's)
Icing sugar is granulated sugar ground to a very fine powder. When mixed with liquid or into butter or cream cheese, it creates a sweet glaze or icing, plus it can be sifted over cakes and desserts. Unless specified, use pure icing sugar, not icing sugar mixture, which contains cornflour (cornstarch) and needs more liquid.

raw (golden) caster
Light brown in colour and honey-like in flavour, raw sugar is slightly less refined than white sugar, with a larger granule. It lends a more pronounced flavour and colour to baked goods. You can use demerara sugar in its place.

sumac
These dried berries of a flowering plant are ground to produce an acidic, vibrant crimson powder that's popular in the Middle East. Sumac has a lemony flavour and is great sprinkled on salads, dips, yoghurt and chicken. Find it at supermarkets and specialty spice shops.

sunflower seeds
These small grey kernels from the black and white seeds of sunflowers are mostly processed for their oil. The kernels are also found in snack mixes and muesli, and can be baked into breads and slices. Buy sunflower seeds in supermarkets.

tahini
A thick paste made from ground sesame seeds, tahini is widely used in Middle-Eastern cooking. It's available in jars and cans from supermarkets and health food stores, in both hulled and unhulled varieties. The recipes in this book call for hulled tahini, for its lighter flavour and smoother texture.

tomato
paste
This triple-concentrated tomato purée is used as a flavour booster and thickener in soups, sauces and stews.

purée (passata)
Italian for 'passed', passata is made by removing the skins and seeds from ripe tomatoes and passing the flesh through a sieve to make a thick, rich tomato purée. You can substitute with sugo, which is made from crushed tomatoes so it has a little more texture than passata. Both are available in bottles from supermarkets.

semi sundried
Sold in jars, stored in oil, or available to buy from supermarkets and delicatessens, semi-dried tomatoes are plump and still a little juicy.

Thai lime leaves
Also known as kaffir or makrut lime, these fragrant leaves have a distinctive double-leaf structure. Commonly crushed or shredded and used as a garnish, the leaves are available fresh or dried, from some supermarkets, most greengrocers and at Asian food stores. Fresh leaves are more flavourful and freeze well.

tofu
Not all tofu is created equal. The recipes in this book call for either firm or silken tofu, which can be found in the chilled section of the supermarket. Where possible, choose organic non-GMO tofu. All brands vary in texture and taste, so don't give up until you find one you love. It's a great source of protein and acts like a sponge for flavour.

tortilla
A thin, unleavened, round flatbread that is a popular vessel for tacos, quesadillas and other Mexican dishes, as well as for wraps. Traditionally made from corn flour, nowadays, wheat flour is often used to make flour tortillas.

vanilla
bean paste
This store-bought paste is a convenient way to replace whole vanilla beans and is great in desserts. One teaspoon of paste substitutes for one vanilla bean.

beans
These fragrant cured pods from the vanilla orchid are used whole, often split with the tiny seeds inside scraped into the mixture to infuse flavour into cream-based recipes.

extract
For a pure vanilla taste, use a good-quality vanilla extract, not an essence or imitation flavour. Vanilla extract features a rounded, rich vanilla flavour.

vinegar
apple cider
With a golden amber colour and a sour appley flavour, this is great for dressings, marinades and chutneys. The recipes in this book call for organic or unfiltered apple cider vinegar.

balsamic
There are many balsamics on the market, ranging in quality and flavour. Aged varieties are preferable. A milder white version is also available, which is used where colour is important.

rice wine
Made from fermenting rice (or rice wine), this is milder and sweeter than vinegars that are made by oxidising distilled wine or other alcohol made from grapes. It's available in white, black, brown and red varieties and can be found in supermarkets and Asian food stores.

wine
Both red and white wine can be distilled into vinegar. Use in dressings, glazes and preserved condiments such as pickles. Use it to make a classic French vinaigrette.

wasabi paste
We know this Japanese paste for its powdery green colour and its heat. Similar to (and most likely containing) horseradish, wasabi paste is used as an ingredient and popular condiment for sushi. It's sold, usually in tubes, at Asian grocers and supermarkets.

yoghurt, natural Greek-style
Recipes in this book call for natural, unsweetened full-fat Greek-style (thick) yoghurt. Check the label for any unwanted sweeteners or artificial flavours.

global measures

Measures vary from Europe to the US and even from Australia to New Zealand.

metric and imperial

Measuring cups and spoons may vary slightly from one country to another, but the difference is generally not sufficient to affect a recipe. The recipes in this book use Australian measures. All cup and spoon measures are level. An Australian measuring cup holds 250ml (8½ fl oz).

One Australian metric teaspoon holds 5ml (⅛ fl oz), one Australian tablespoon holds 20ml (¾ fl oz) (4 teaspoons). However, in the USA, New Zealand and the UK, 15ml (½ fl oz) (3-teaspoon) tablespoons are used.

When measuring dry ingredients, add the ingredient loosely to the cup and level with a knife. Don't tap or shake to compact the ingredient unless the recipe requests 'firmly packed'.

liquids and solids

Measuring cups, spoons and scales are great assets in the kitchen – these equivalents are a guide.

liquids

cup	metric	imperial
⅛ cup	30ml	1 fl oz
¼ cup	60ml	2 fl oz
⅓ cup	80ml	2¾ fl oz
½ cup	125ml	4¼ fl oz
⅔ cup	160ml	5½ fl oz
¾ cup	180ml	6 fl oz
1 cup	250ml	8½ fl oz
2 cups	500ml	17 fl oz
3 cups	750ml	25 fl oz
4 cups	1 litre	34 fl oz

solids

metric	imperial
20g	¾ oz
60g	2 oz
125g	4½ oz
180g	6¼ oz
250g	8¾ oz
450g	1 lb
750g	1 lb 10 oz
1kg	2 lb 3 oz

more equivalents

Here are a few more simplified equivalents for metric and imperial measures, plus ingredient names.

millimetres to inches

metric	imperial
3mm	⅛ inch
6mm	¼ inch
1cm	½ inch
2.5cm	1 inch
5cm	2 inches
18cm	7 inches
20cm	8 inches
23cm	9 inches
25cm	10 inches
30cm	12 inches

ingredient equivalents

almond meal	ground almonds
bicarbonate of soda	baking soda
caster sugar	superfine sugar
celeriac	celery root
chickpeas	garbanzo beans
coriander	cilantro
cornflour	cornstarch
cos lettuce	romaine lettuce
eggplant	aubergine
gai lan	chinese broccoli
green onion	scallion
icing sugar	confectioner's sugar
plain flour	all-purpose flour
rocket	arugula
self-raising flour	self-rising flour
silverbeet	swiss chard
snow pea	mange tout
white sugar	granulated sugar
zucchini	courgette

oven temperatures

Setting the oven to the correct temperature can be crucial when baking sweet things.

celsius to fahrenheit

celsius	fahrenheit
100°C	200°F
120°C	250°F
140°C	275°F
150°C	300°F
160°C	325°F
180°C	350°F
190°C	375°F
200°C	400°F
220°C	425°F

electric to gas

celsius	gas
110°C	¼
130°C	½
140°C	1
150°C	2
170°C	3
180°C	4
190°C	5
200°C	6
220°C	7
230°C	8
240°C	9
250°C	10

butter and eggs

Let 'fresh is best' be your mantra when it comes to selecting eggs and dairy goods.

butter

We generally use unsalted butter as it allows for a little more control over a recipe's flavour. Either way, the impact is minimal. Salted butter has a longer shelf life and is preferred by some people. One American stick of butter is 125g (4½ oz). One Australian block of butter is 250g (8¾ oz).

eggs

Unless otherwise indicated, we use large (60g/2 oz) chicken eggs. To preserve freshness, store eggs in the refrigerator in the carton they are sold in. Use only the freshest eggs in recipes such as mayonnaise or dressings that use raw or barely cooked eggs. Be extra cautious if there is a salmonella problem in your community, particularly with food that is to be served to children, pregnant women or the elderly.

useful weights

Here are a few simple weight conversions for cupfuls of commonly used ingredients.

common ingredients

almond meal (ground almonds)
1 cup | 120g | 4¼ oz

brown sugar
1 cup | 240g | 8½ oz

raw caster (superfine) sugar
1 cup | 220g | 7¾ oz

coconut sugar
1 cup | 150g | 5¼ oz

desiccated coconut
1 cup | 80g | 2¾ oz

**plain (all-purpose)
or self-raising (self-rising) flour**
1 cup | 150g | 5¼ oz

fresh sourdough breadcrumbs
1 cup | 70g | 2½ oz

raw or roasted cashews
1 cup | 150g | 5¼ oz

plain thick yoghurt
1 cup | 250g | 9 oz

uncooked brown rice
1 cup | 200g | 7 oz

cooked brown rice
1 cup | 165g | 5¾ oz

cooked quinoa
1 cup | 140g | 5 oz

fresh or frozen berries
1 cup | 125g | 4½ oz

thank you

Those of you who know me would understand that I am no stranger to creating a cookbook. However, I am definitely not alone in bringing this book to life. It's a little team of hardworking and talented individuals who all excel in what they do and have helped make this book amazing.

To my right-hand wonder woman, Hannah Schubert, the ultimate backup dancer – designer, producer, recipe editor, recipe taster, scheduler and the one who keeps things moving (and the best barista EVER!). You are truly a superstar!

To the lovely Con Poulos. Thank you for creating such magical images.

Thanks to Genevieve for a beautiful design, sunny colours and your too-easy attitude.

To my editor, Pru. A very big thank you for whipping this book into shape.

To the kitchen whiz, Jacinta Cannataci. These recipes are so incredible because of your unfailing attention to detail. Thank you for testing everything to perfection.

Thank you to William and Liv for your 'anything is possible' attitude and for keeping us rolling along at pace.

Many thanks to my publisher, Catherine Milne, for the many book development cookie meetings. Your sugar levels can now return to a normal range (for a while anyway)! To the rest of my team at HarperCollins – Jim, Scott, Shannon and Janelle – thank you for your enthusiasm and support.

My sincerest thanks to the creative ceramicists Marjoke De Heer (@marjokedeheer), Angela Nicholson (@angela_nicholson_studio), Mud Australia (@mudaustralia) and Mennt (@madebymennt). Your pieces have brought such beauty to this book.

To my partners at Miele. Your appliances are an absolute joy to cook, bake, grill, stir-fry and test countless numbers of recipes with. I so appreciate your support.

Thank you Ross and Dan at Hale Imports for my beautiful knives (@shun.australia).

My heartfelt thanks also to the dh team, who work behind the scenes to keep the dh world turning: Karen, Natalie and Allison, I couldn't do it without you.

Last but not at all least, the biggest thank you to my amazing partner and my boys. Your support and love is everything to me. And your understanding around 'book season'! To my family and my amazing friends, thank you endlessly.

And to all of you who buy my books, follow my videos and social media, visit my website and purchase my dh products. None of this would be possible without you, and for that I am truly grateful.

More books to love

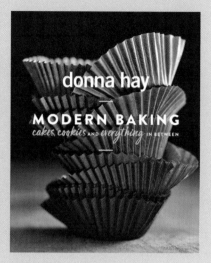

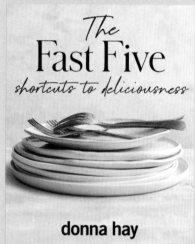

Connect with Donna
anytime, anywhere...

for videos, recipes, homewares, inspiration and more...
visit the donna hay website.

www.donnahay.com

about
Donna

As Australia's leading food editor and best-selling cookbook author, Donna Hay has made her way into hearts (and countless homes) across the globe.

An international publishing phenomenon, Donna's name is synonymous with accessible yet inspirational recipes, her distinctively elegant and globally recognised styling and stunning images. Her acclaimed magazine notched up an incredible 100 issues and her best-selling cookbooks have sold more than eight million copies worldwide.

The donna hay brand goes beyond the printed page, featuring an impressive digital presence, a number of television series (her latest is streaming on Disney+), branded merchandise, and a baking mix range.

Donna adores living near the ocean with her partner and boys and still loves cooking every single day.